THE COUNTRY GIRL

Also by Clifford Odets

AWAKE AND SING

WAITING FOR LEFTY

TILL THE DAY I DIE

PARADISE LOST

THE SILENT PARTNER
(unproduced)

GOLDEN BOY

THE LAW OF FLIGHT
(unproduced)

ROCKET TO THE MOON

NIGHT MUSIC

CLASH BY NIGHT

THE BIG KNIFE

THE

Country Girl

A PLAY
IN THREE ACTS
BY

Clifford Odets

NEW YORK
THE VIKING PRESS
1951

PRINTED IN U.S.A. BY
AMERICAN BOOK–KNICKERBOCKER PRESS, INC., NEW YORK

FOR BETTE.

THE COUNTRY GIRL

≫-≫≫-≫≫-≫≫≪-≪≪-≪≪-≪

Cast of Characters

BERNIE DODD : a director
LARRY : a stage manager
PHIL COOK : a producer
PAUL UNGER : an author
NANCY STODDARD : an ingénue
FRANK ELGIN : an actor
GEORGIE ELGIN : his wife
RALPH : a dresser

Synopsis of Scenes

THE ACTION IS CONTEMPORARY

ACT ONE

SCENE 1 : The stage of a New York theater.
SCENE 2 : A furnished room, later the same day.
SCENE 3 : The rehearsal stage, ten days later.
SCENE 4 : The furnished room, a week later.
SCENE 5 : A dressing room in a Boston theater, after midnight, a week later.

ACT TWO

SCENE 1 : The Boston dressing room, a few nights later.
SCENE 2 : The Boston dressing room, the next day.
SCENE 3 : A dressing room in a New York theater, evening, some weeks later.

*Throughout the play, in the stage directions,
right and left mean stage right and stage left.*

THE COUNTRY GIRL

ACT ONE: *Scene 1*

>>->>>->>>->>>->>>->>>->>>->>>->>>->>>->>>->>)(((-(((-(((-(((-(((-(((-(((-(((-(((-(((-(((-((

In a muted gloomy atmosphere three men are seated or stand-
ing on the bare stage of a New York theater. The stage is set
for a rehearsal; chairs are strewn about in an order which
indicates the demarcation of a set. There is a work table at
the left. A pilot light and a strip provide the illumination.

  Soft radio music, a popular Mexican song handled by a
lamenting but insinuating tenor, comes from one side. Bernie
Dodd, the director, is softly whistling with the song. Paul
Unger, the playwright, has straddled a chair, his back to the
audience. The producer, Phil Cook, is gravely and thought-
fully smoking a Turkish cigarette. It is very evident that the
men have something on their minds.

BERNIE, *looking intently at Cook, to no one in particular:*
Where's that music coming from? *No one answers. Bernie*
pauses before sauntering down to Cook. Well, what about it?
Cook's face tightens and he won't answer. Larry, the stage
manager, comes in from the right and respectfully addresses
Bernie.

LARRY: Do you want me to hold the company, Bernie? They're
waiting.

BERNIE: Dismiss them, no. But tell them to stand by for a possible seven o'clock call tonight.

LARRY: Right. *He starts out but stops as Bernie speaks.*

BERNIE: Elgin, I want Elgin to wait.

LARRY: Frank Elgin?

BERNIE: Yes, have him wait. Where's that music coming from?

LARRY: Prop man's room.

BERNIE: Oh . . .

Larry leaves.

BERNIE, *to Cook:* Well, what's the verdict?

COOK, *in a low voice:* I wish I could lay myself away in a safety deposit box for a few months!

Bernie snorts, not impolitely. Unger turns and represses a yawn. Cook looks painfully and resentfully at Bernie.

COOK: Bernie, you get the damnedest ideas of any man I ever met!

BERNIE, *quietly:* I'm as annoyed as you are, Phil, but a little realism is of the essence, to quote one of your favorite lines.

COOK: But what the heck's realistic about giving Elgin a reading? Am I dumb? Why not let the doorman read for the part?

Nancy, a young ingénue, enters very timidly from the right.

BERNIE, *sternly:* Don't come in here, Nancy—we're busy.

NANCY: I'm awfully sorry, Mr. Dodd. I left my part on the chair. May I?

Bernie nods impatiently and watches Nancy as she takes her part and leaves, saying, "Please excuse me, everyone."

COOK, *fumingly:* Damn it, Bernie, I don't follow you and that's the truth!

BERNIE, *coldly:* What don't you follow? We've been in rehearsal four days. *Sarcastically:* Due to a technical fluke with the contract—not your fault, of course—Mr. Billy Hertz, our leading man, is on his way to Hollywood and a flowery two-picture deal. As of today, here and now, we are minus a leading man. Since we are booked into Boston on the twenty-eighth we are in trouble.

COOK, *impatiently:* I know all of this.

BERNIE: Then let me read Elgin for the part. Twelve years ago I saw him give two performances that made my hair stand up— *Abruptly he calls offstage:* Close that door and keep it closed! *To Cook, angrily:* Cookie, don't you understand? All I'm saying is let me read him for the part!

UNGER, *quietly:* That's right, Phil. It doesn't do any harm to give the man a reading.

COOK, *after a pause, shrugging:* All right, read him—I don't say don't read him.

Bernie, annoyed, prowls around the stage.

BERNIE: But don't make any cracks when I call him in.

COOK: But I happen to remember you looked this Elgin up five weeks ago for the part. He didn't do then and he won't do now.

BERNIE: But I gave him the general understudy, didn't I?

COOK: Proving what?

BERNIE: Proving I didn't think his whole future was behind him.

Cook mutters something.

BERNIE: What?

COOK: Nothing . . .

Bernie looks at him and then abruptly swings off to the right.

BERNIE, *calling offstage:* Larry . . . Larry! *Larry appears at the right.* Ask Frank Elgin to come in, kid.

Disgusted, Cook grinds his cigarette underfoot; he is always gloomy, with a certain heavy pout about him, always dependent and uncertain of himself, but never wanting to admit it. Unger is thirty, tender-hearted and open, simple in a good sense.

Bernie Dodd can be very direct; he is small but with lots of wiry and graceful physical energy. At just thirty-five he is very successful, somewhat fretful and prowling when in rehearsal. Normally, however, his manner is friendly if a little watchful. From former excess of feeling about any and all things he has become saturnine, his face impassive; there is a gloomy, thoughtful overtone about him. This gives him an air of unwillingness, as if he no longer wants to be personally involved with persons or things; actually it is a form of protective distrust, expressing itself in what seems a main quality of being objective and impersonal, as if one were working with a screw driver on a cold piece of machinery. But, of course, this mask of impersonality is not the truth. Just now Bernie is typically prowling.

Larry returns with Frank Elgin, an actor of fifty, whose present seediness does not hide a certain distinction of personality. He is nervous but nevertheless deports himself like the important actor he used to be. He stands there awkwardly, quite aware that three pairs of eyes are searching him.

FRANK: You want me, Mr. Dodd?

BERNIE: Yeah, Frank, sit down a minute. *To Larry:* Company dismissed?

LARRY: Yes, sir.

BERNIE: Frank, I want you to do something for me. Not so much for me as for our producer and Mr. Unger, the author. Read the part of Judge Murray for them.

FRANK: Billy Hertz *is* out for good, huh?

BERNIE, *ignoring his remark:* Not that I can promise anything.

FRANK, *puzzled and nervous:* Why do you want *me* to read?

COOK, *darkly:* Why does someone want you to read a part?

BERNIE, *abruptly calling off to the left:* Hey, "Props"! Shut off that radio or close the door! *Gently, to Frank:* Read the part, Frank.

FRANK: Sure . . . All right . . .

He stands, but his attitude seems so slow and reluctant that it annoys Cook. The music disappears.

COOK: Of course, you wouldn't take the part if we offered it to you, would you?

FRANK, *humbly:* I'm not fighting, Mr. Cook. If you want me to read for you . . .

BERNIE, *to Larry:* The disclosure scene, end of Act Two. Find the place for him and wait outside, kid.

COOK: Everyone in the theater is slightly bats in the belfry!

LARRY: Don't want me to cue him in?

Larry has picked up the script and now hands Frank the actual part. Bernie, annoyed with Cook, takes the script from Larry.

BERNIE: No, I'll do it.

Larry finds the place, hands the part back to Frank, and goes. Part in hand, Frank seems momentarily helpless as he crosses and elaborately drops his cigarette into a pail.

BERNIE: Take it easy, Frank. I'm not looking for a performance. Sit, walk, anything you want. Got the place?

FRANK, *hefts the part in his hand, attempting humor:* Yes. Feels like the Sunday *Times*.

BERNIE: We can cut down to—Bert is already in—the Judge's line: "I didn't ask you to sit down . . ."

Trying to hide his agitation, Frank paces, looking upward for the best light by which to read.

FRANK: "I didn't ask you to sit down . . . because I don't want a louse on my furniture." That it?

BERNIE: Yes. *Continuing in the play:* "I don't think this furniture will be yours much longer, Judge Murray!"

FRANK: "And I think I'll have to ask for an explanation of this big-mouth attitude. You damn Reform Party kids come and go like a ten-cent piece of ice. Now get out before I kick you out! You only got in here because you know Ellen!"

BERNIE: "I resent that!"

FRANK: "Not as much as I—" *He moves nervously under the lights.* What is that? I can't make it out. *Then:* Oh! "Not as much as I resent you, you little Wop bastard!"

BERNIE: "I'm not letting you put this discussion on any personal plane! There's too much at stake!"

FRANK, *as Bernie begins to read the same line:* "I represent the collective will of thousands of our best—"

BERNIE: No, that's my line, Frank.

FRANK, *lamely:* Well, it's in this part. I can't see what I'm reading. I mean the light—I mean—Hertz is got the whole part penciled up.

BERNIE, *urgently:* Go on, don't stop.

FRANK: I can't. I'm sorry. I'm saying, "Hands, behave!" but they're shaking like a leaf.

BERNIE: Start right from where we left off.

Frank looks at Bernie and Cook from under his eyebrows, not lifting his head; then he drops his eyes and slowly shakes his head.

BERNIE: What's the matter?

FRANK: It won't do, Mr. Dodd. I always was a dead bunny when it came to sight reading. Thanks for the chance, but it won't do.

He walks to a table with bitter dignity and puts the part down. Cook enjoys this part of the scene. Bernie is annoyed.

BERNIE, *to Unger:* Give him a clean script, Paul.

FRANK, *unhappily:* What's the use? You've been very nice, Dodd. You looked me up before—gave me the general understudy— I appreciate what you did, but—

BERNIE, *abruptly calling offstage:* Dammit, I want that door shut and stay shut! *He throws the script to the table and turns.* I can't be that wrong, Frank— I know an actor when I see one! Let's forget the damn script! Let's improvise the scene! Just the situation—not the author's scene!

FRANK: How do you mean?

BERNIE: Ad lib, just ad lib it. Improvise it. Look at me! I'm a fresh kid—I wanna marry your grandchild and you don't want me to. That's the situation. *He begins to pace, waving the others aside. Soon he is pacing around Frank, like a bull fighter around a helpless animal, which is the impression*

Frank gives for the moment. Then, angrily: "I don't leave this house until I get your answer. Don't call in any servants or I'll knock them all on their ears!"

FRANK, *slowly:* "What . . . do you want?"

BERNIE: "I want to marry your grandchild and you don't want me to!"

FRANK: "Why should I let you marry my grandchild?" *Anxiously:* Right? *Then:* "Who the hell are you to come busting in this house like a hurricane?"

BERNIE: "You don't answer phones, so I'm here in person!"

They are gradually slipping into a really dramatic scene, Frank standing stock still until, in a moment, he begins to follow Bernie wherever he moves; shortly they begin banging on the table.

FRANK: "I usually make up my own mind when and when not to answer the phone. As far as Ellen's concerned, as far as she's concerned—you can go to hell!"

BERNIE: "You won't talk to me that way again!"

FRANK: "I'll talk to you that way again and again and again!" Is that what you want? *Suddenly choleric:* "Now get out before I open your head with a poker!"

BERNIE: "We have to have a talk, a long talk, Frank."

FRANK, *dropping his voice:* "I'll talk, I'll talk to you, son. Let's see what's really on your mind."

BERNIE, *tauntingly:* "I don't think you can stop me, Frank!"

FRANK, *scornfully:* "Oh, I'll stop you! I'll stop you, Dodd, if it's the last thing I do! Don't underestimate me. I haven't begun to fight yet. And—"

BERNIE: "I'm sorry for you! By next week you'll be front-page news!"

FRANK, *angrily:* "Wait a minute, wait a minute! What the devil are you talking about? Explain this thing to me!"

BERNIE: "I'm head of the Citizens' Non-Partisan Committee, too."

Frank, really acting now, looks at him incredulously and then abruptly bursts into laughter. He breaks that up with a fit of coughing.

FRANK: "Did you ever tell that to Ellen?"

BERNIE: "I'm telling her tonight."

FRANK, *chortling:* "Well, boy, that's just what I want you to do! God Almighty, I want you to tell her your plans! I want to be behind a door when you tell her your plans!"

BERNIE, *quickly:* That's it, Frank! Now change the color. You've lost everything. Where is Ellen—you haven't seen her for two days—she's deserted you.

FRANK, *changing to a pensive thoughtfulness:* "Ellen? Where's Ellen? Haven't seen her for two days . . ." *He has seated himself, but now he slowly stands, shakes his head, shows worry and nervousness for the first time.* "Is . . . my daughter in the house?" *He turns and moves around like an old man.* "I have the greatest confidence in her!" *Scornfully:* "Now I think I asked you to get out of here about a long moment ago!"

The two men are standing, facing each other. Now, after a pause, Bernie drops out of the scene.

BERNIE, *admiringly:* That's it, Frank! That's the way you used to go!

But Frank, as Bernie glances triumphantly at Cook and Unger, continues the scene with strength and bitterness, flinging his overcoat in Bernie's face.

FRANK: "Now get out of here! Don't look at me that way. Nobody wants your pity or your help. It's no satisfaction in a cold world to have your colder pity! Werba was a great man in his day—that's what all the loafers are saying. Werba made his millions, but the boy wonder is living with his in-laws now, they say! And now you come here and tell me, 'Mr. Werba, you're going to prison within the month.' Well, let me tell you—Werba won't give up his name and take a number! Werba is still a great man! He tore an empire out of the world before he was thirty and he'll live to do it again! And when that time comes—you listen to this!—I won't forget my enemies or my friends. I will never forget those who dragged me down!"

Frank has been talking directly front to Bernie, who has seated himself at the table, his back to the theater. Now Frank sighs deeply, breaking a strange spell of majesty.

BERNIE: That was the last speech of *Werba's Millions*, wasn't it?

FRANK: Yes . . . *Standing, he rubs his hands and shakes his head, as if he were dizzy. He gives the impression of slowly waking into a colder, shabbier world.* It came back to me . . .

BERNIE, *glancing briefly at the others, gently to Frank:* Frank, would you wait outside for me? Two minutes, in one of the dressing rooms, please.

FRANK: Yes, I'll wait . . .

He goes off to the right. Bernie joins the others, repressing his satisfaction.

BERNIE: Well, what did you see?

UNGER: If you're asking me, something I wouldn't have believed. Where was that seedy guy hiding all that power and majesty?

COOK: We've done three shows together—Bernie, I know you well. You're a man of violent preconceptions.

BERNIE: Didn't that scene speak for itself?

COOK: What did it speak? Does five minutes of ad lib prove he can memorize and play eighty sides? Just bear in mind this is for a potent seventy thousand bucks! He's been laying in pickle for a good ten years!

BERNIE, *quietly:* Someone took a chance one day with an actress named Laurette Taylor—and look what she did in her last few years.

COOK: But, darling, that man's a bleary bum!

BERNIE: I don't want him to hear you—don't raise your voice. *He waits a moment. Then:* Well, what about him?

COOK: Look, you own twenty per cent of this show *yourself!* *To Unger:* You're the playwright—doesn't this worry *you?*

UNGER, *promptly:* Not if it doesn't worry Bernie.

COOK, *momentarily stymied, hesitates before turning:* What about Ray Newton? He's still available.

BERNIE, *sharply:* I don't want Ray Newton! He's my idea of nothing, just nothing!

COOK: Well, what do you think you can get out of *him?*

BERNIE, *flatly:* I don't know.

COOK, *aghast:* You don't know?

BERNIE: How the hell should I know? *He makes a mark in the air.* He's a big dark X! *Prowling again.* Do you think I underestimate the job if I use this lush?

UNGER, *smiling to himself:* Don't raise your voice.

BERNIE: We open in Boston in three weeks and two days. I'll have to manipulate and outthink him every inch of the way. *He snorts.* Big comfort—my father was a lush—I have some background for the job. *He turns to Unger.* But if this comes off you're apt to get something that happens once in twenty years!

UNGER, *impressed:* I believe you if you say so.

COOK: And he's apt to have an ulcerated sponge for a brain, too.

BERNIE: We can stay out till he's letter perfect. The season's young.

COOK: But I'm not!

BERNIE: Then what do you want to do? Postpone? *Answering his own question:* Postpone!

COOK, *dismayed:* How can we postpone? We're in for a twenty-thousand-dollar bite already. The scenery's ordered, the guarantees on the house—

BERNIE, *swiftly:* Then what do you want to do?

COOK, *hesitantly:* Could we . . . look around for someone else while he's rehearsing?

BERNIE, *firmly:* No, I won't do that. Once we start we don't let him go without real cause. A binge is real cause. Or if he can't retain lines. And, hold your hat, I wanna give him a run-of-the-play contract, not a two weeks' deal. *Quickly:* Because I'd

need his complete confidence, Cookie. Give him a two weeks'
deal and he knows we can let him out any time.

Cook, *indignantly:* No, sir! No run-of-the-play contract for
Mr. Elgin. I'd rather go back to Dallas and—

He starts out, but Bernie takes him by an arm and turns him.

Bernie, *quietly:* Okay, Phil—two weeks' deal.

Cook, *disturbed, after a pause:* What do we pay him?

Bernie: A few hundred a week.

*A pause. Cook agrees by not answering. The prop man must
have opened his door, for the music begins again.*

Bernie, *warningly:* But I mean it, Phil—I don't let him out
without real cause.

Cook: Umm . . .

Bernie, *turning:* Agreed with you, Paul?

Unger: Umm . . .

*Poised, as if a dancer, Bernie's eyes and manner begin to
sparkle; his attitude is tense but quietly expressive.*

Bernie: I'm one of those fools who saw Laurette Taylor in
The Glass Menagerie eight times. Now . . . maybe something
here . . . I'm not saying what . . . but it needs your real co-
operation. *He walks over to the right and calls:* Frank! Frank
Elgin! Oh, Frank!

*Larry enters from the right as Bernie begins prowling ex-
pectantly.*

Larry: You want Mr. Elgin?

Bernie, *walking back:* Yes, send him in.

LARRY: He's gone—he left.

BERNIE: What do you mean, he left?

LARRY: He left about five minutes ago.

BERNIE, *impatiently:* Where? Coffee? What?

LARRY: He just walked out, Bernie. He didn't say.

Bernie's face grows grim; behind him Cook smirks.

BERNIE: I see I'll have to go and get him. *Pausing, glowering, Bernie turns abruptly and hurries out.*

COOK, *bitterly:* He's going to go and get him! In what Eighth Avenue bar? *Wagging his head, Cook starts out, Unger following.*

Curtain

ACT ONE: *Scene 2*

>>>->>>->>>->>>->>>->>>->>>->>>->>>->>>->>>->XX<-<<<-<<<-<<<-<<<-<<<-<<<-<<<-<<<-<<<-<<<-<<

*Frank's furnished room in mid-Manhattan, west of Eighth
Avenue, a little later. The shabby room is lighted by a lamp
and a small window; it is not possible to tell that it is high
noon outside. In the center is an iron bedstead. To the right,
a chest and a wardrobe. Downstage right, a kitchenette in an
alcove. The door is also at the right. Loud music comes out of
a small radio. Frank's wife, Georgie Elgin, is obviously doing
two things—suffering from a toothache and packing a suitcase.
She turns at a knock at the door.*

GEORGIE: Yes, yes, I'll turn it down . . . *Instead she turns the
radio off completely. Numb and listless, she returns to pick
up and examine a dress on a hanger. She is surprised when
the knocking starts again; she stands, thinks, and finally asks:*
Who is it?

BERNIE'S VOICE: Is Mr. Elgin in?

GEORGIE: Just a minute . . . *She stuffs the dress into the suitcase, closes it hastily, and pushes it under the bed; she smooths
out the top of the bed. Warily she walks to the door and opens
it.* Yes . . . ?

BERNIE, *in the doorway:* Is Mr. Elgin in?

GEORGIE: No. I don't know when he'll be back.

BERNIE: Are you Mrs. Elgin? *She nods.* I wanted to talk to
Frank.

GEORGIE: I don't know when he'll be back—he's rehearsing—in a show, you know.

BERNIE, *briskly:* I'll wait—it's important.

Bernie has pushed past her and is inside, looking at the room. She looks at him rather stupidly; and only when he looks at her does she seem to come to with a start.

GEORGIE: I was just going to make some coffee . . . *Vaguely beginning this business, she looks back, wondering who Bernie is. She says to make talk:* Is it raining hard outside?

BERNIE: It isn't raining.

GEORGIE: Isn't . . . ? Felt as if it were. It's cold out . . . the summer collapsed so abruptly, didn't it? You could fall asleep here and not wake up till they called you for the Judgment Day.

BERNIE, *who has been making notes in a small book:* What do I smell, incense?

GEORGIE: It cuts the restaurant odors from down below.

BERNIE: I think I'd rather have the restaurant.

GEORGIE: It always comes in such spooky flavors, Sandalwood, Wisteria—this one's called Cobra.

BERNIE: I guess it's supposed to kill you. *He snorts.*

GEORGIE, *smiles, then abruptly winces:* Does my face look swollen?

BERNIE: No.

GEORGIE: I have a bad toothache. All of autumn's in this tooth. *She approaches Bernie.* You don't look like one of Frank's friends.

BERNIE: I'm the director of the play he's working in.

GEORGIE: Oh! You're what's-his-name?

BERNIE: Bernie Dodd.

GEORGIE, *staring at him:* Dodd . . . You're even younger than I thought, from what I've read and heard.

BERNIE, *archly:* In this spot, most people would put in a flattering word.

GEORGIE: I amuse you, don't I?

BERNIE: No, but you act like an old lady and you're not.

GEORGIE, *seeing him looking impatiently at his watch, crosses and picks up a clock:* What time is it?

BERNIE: Twenty minutes to twelve.

GEORGIE: Three clocks, a radio, and never know the time. *She turns.* Twenty after twelve?

Bernie, crossing to look at a framed photo, corrects her. She sets the clock and puts it down.

BERNIE: That's a good photograph of Frank. Recent?

GEORGIE: No, that's a very long time ago—the year we were married. We went out to Hollywood that year.

BERNIE, *surprised:* Was Frank ever in pictures?

GEORGIE: For a year or two, but it was spooky. People were endlessly kind, but it never worked out and we came back. *Of another photo, sarcastically:* That's my father. I come from Hartford. No, I won't, thanks. *She refuses one of Bernie's cigarettes. Crossing, she picks up a small bottle of hand lotion and rubs the lotion into her hands.* Isn't it strange—I thought it was raining. My hands are numb.

BERNIE: Does Frank usually come right home?

GEORGIE: Unless he sits out on the brownstone stoop. *Abruptly:* Is something wrong?

BERNIE: Does Frank still drink?

GEORGIE, *with sudden alert evasion:* Just like us—one mouth and five fingers on every hand. *Seeing his arch look:* What did you think I'd answer, Mr. Dodd?

BERNIE: Touché.

GEORGIE, *not hearing:* What?

BERNIE: Touché. That means—

GEORGIE, *cutting him off:* Oh, come, everyone knows what touché means.

BERNIE, *faintly annoyed:* What are we doing here, jockeying for position? *He jabs a finger at some books.* Who reads these books?

GEORGIE, *coldly now:* I borrow them on a library card.

BERNIE: Balzac, Dreiser, Jane Austen . . . *He smiles.* I'm afraid to ask you if you enjoy them—you'll bite my head off.

GEORGIE, *intently:* I enjoy them. But I'd like to know what you're doing here. You're making me very nervous and I don't like it. What is this about Frank?

Frank walks in and stops when he sees Bernie; a very direct man and a very indirect man are looking at each other.

BERNIE: What happened to you?

FRANK: I decided to walk . . .

BERNIE: I asked you to wait.

FRANK, *after a pause:* Any coffee, Georgie? Make some coffee . . .

Georgie crosses to the cooking coffee pot, keeping her eyes on Frank.

BERNIE: I'm a busy man, Frank.

FRANK, *uneasily:* What do you want me to do?

BERNIE: Make up your mind—I want you to play that part.

GEORGIE: I'm an innocent bystander. Don't shoot me—just tell me what this is all about.

FRANK: Mr. Dodd says he wants me to play the lead in his play . . .

BERNIE, *briskly, annoyed:* It's a starring part that needs an actor who can stay sober and learn lines. Are you that actor or not?

FRANK, *with flare:* Well, I'm not one of those goddamn microphone actors like Billy Hertz! I'm an actor!

BERNIE, *waiting:* That's what I used to think.

FRANK, *evasively:* What about the producer? If looks would kill, I was dead.

BERNIE: He's afraid you're a drinker.

FRANK, *sullenly:* I don't drink on a show.

BERNIE, *sharply:* Not according to Gilbert. I checked with him—you worked with him in '44? What happened?

FRANK, *looks at Georgie before answering:* We lost our little daughter . . . that year.

Silence. Frank sits on the bed. Georgie pours the coffee.

BERNIE, *quietly:* Can you stay on the wagon now?

FRANK, *after a pause:* Look, son, I think we oughta forget it—

BERNIE: Don't call me son! You've played bigger parts—you used to be a star!

FRANK, *gloomily:* Yeah, I used to drink a glass of money for breakfast, too.

BERNIE, *angrily:* What's the matter with you?

GEORGIE, *as if waking up:* You don't listen, Mr. Dodd. Don't you see he's afraid of the responsibility?

BERNIE: But I'm willing to take a chance—the gamble's all on *my* side.

FRANK, *expostulating uneasily:* Why kid around? They open in Boston the twenty-eighth. I couldn't even learn the lines in that time! That part needs a Bennett or a Blinn—

BERNIE, *sardonically:* Bad enough to go to Hollywood to cast—now you suggest I go to heaven! *He stares at them coldly; about to walk out, he turns and says earnestly:* Listen, Frank, you don't know me. But I was a kid when I saw you give two great performances in mediocre plays—*Proud People* and *Werba's Millions*. I can get the same show out of you right now—if you lay off the liquor! I have more confidence in you than you have in yourself!

GEORGIE, *sitting back and watching:* Why?

BERNIE: Because I saw him as a kid—I was a hat-check boy in the Shubert theaters. *To Frank:* You and Lunt and Walter Huston—you were my heroes. I know everything you did.

FRANK: Hear that, Georgie?

GEORGIE, *with quiet thoughtfulness:* Naturally, Mr. Dodd, you exaggerate the sentiment to make your point.

BERNIE, *looking at her very carefully:* We killed the cat with sentiment? Okay, we'll bring him back to life with some antiseptic truth. I come from realistic people—I'm Italian. *He pauses.* I'm not blind to Frank's condition—he's a bum! But I'm tough, not one of those nice "humane" people: they hand you a drink and a buck and that's exactly where they stop. *To Frank:* I won't hand you a buck, but I'll think about you, if you take this job. I'll commit myself to you—we'll work and worry together—it's a marriage! And I'll make you work, if you take this job. *I'll be your will! He pauses again.* But if you do me dirt—only once!—no pity, Frank! Not a drop of pity! Joke ending, kid.

Georgie looks more carefully at Bernie. We can almost see her come to life as she steps in closer.

GEORGIE: You'll be his "will"—I like that. That's what he needs, a will. And "no pity"—I like that, too. I like the "antiseptic truth." But what kind of contract do you offer?

BERNIE, *promptly:* Standard two-week contract.

GEORGIE: Not run-of-the-play?

BERNIE: No.

GEORGIE: Doesn't that mean you could let Frank out any time with two weeks' notice?

BERNIE, *impatiently:* That's what it means.

GEORGIE: But suppose he takes the part and opens the show? He gets you over the top of the hill. How does he know you won't replace him?

BERNIE, *with flat indignation:* No run-of-the-play contract. Suppose we have to drop him? For drinking or for not retaining his lines? What do you want? Drop him, replace him, and *still* pay his salary for the run of the show?

GEORGIE, *after a pause:* I don't think he should take it. He needs confidence. He won't have it with that two weeks' clause over his head. Would *you? She has spiked Bernie's guns by presenting to him the same case he previously presented to Cook.*

BERNIE, *finally, after pausing, looking from one to the other:* I have nothing in my mind except for Frank to play this part.

GEORGIE, *as sharply:* That's sentiment again!

BERNIE, *heatedly:* I can't believe my ears! I came up here with the best intentions in the world—now I find I'm victimizing you!

FRANK, *nervously:* May I get a word in edgewise?

BERNIE: What the hell did I do? Bring you a basket of snakes?

GEORGIE, *coldly:* Noblesse oblige, Mr. Dodd. Stop whirling like a dervish.

FRANK: Nobody wants to get your goat, Mr. Dodd. I—what I mean, Mr. Dodd, it's only a matter of not wanting to bite off more than I can chew.

BERNIE, *after a pause, coldly:* You have the offer. We're booked into Boston for two weeks, but the season's young—we can stay out till you're letter perfect.

FRANK, *eagerly:* And . . . would you do that?

BERNIE, *promptly:* Do it? I *insist* upon it! Do I look green? *Looking at Georgie:* I'll take that back—I *am* green! *To Frank:* Call me at the office by three o'clock. That means not later.

He starts out but stops. You need a twenty-dollar bill? You need it . . . *He puts the bill on the radio and goes.*

Silence. Frank does not move.

GEORGIE: Is that boy as talented as he throws himself around?

FRANK, *moodily:* Best average in both the leagues.

GEORGIE: He's willful, but he meant what he said.

FRANK, *turning aside:* I can't do it, can I?

GEORGIE: Doesn't it seem strange for you to ask me that?

FRANK, *unhappily:* You're my wife.

GEORGIE, *quietly:* Frank, we've been through all this before, many times before. I'm tired, Frank.

FRANK, *brooding, not looking at her:* What happened? Where did I get so bolloxed up? I was the best young leading man in this business, not a slouch!

GEORGIE: Scripts didn't come . . .

FRANK: I knew it then—on the coast—I lost my nerve! And then, when we lost the money, in '39, after those lousy Federal Theater jobs—! *He pauses and shakes his head.* This is the face that once turned down radio work. *He paces.* Whatever the hell I did, I don't know what! *Abruptly defiant, he stops behind her.* But I'm good! I'm still good, baby, because I see what *they think* is good! *He waits, but she is silent.* Don't you think I'm good? *I* think I'm good!

GEORGIE, *quietly:* Then take the part. Make it your own responsibility, not mine. Take the part.

He looks at her. It is plain that the idea frightens him.

GEORGIE: Don't wiggle and caper, Frank. *Suddenly:* Can't you admit to yourself you're a failure? You'd die to save your face, not to fail in public—but I'm your wife: you have no face. Try to be clear about this offer—think.

FRANK: I didn't hear him say he'd star me.

GEORGIE, *with dry weariness:* I have a message for you, Frank: take the part!

FRANK: Yes, but what will *you* do if I—?

GEORGIE, *firmly:* Leave me out. Take the part and do your level best. *She slowly rubs a hand against her aching jaw.*

FRANK, *uneasily:* But what about that two weeks' clause? You yourself tried—

GEORGIE: All I tried was to get a better deal. But you won't get perfect terms.

FRANK: You certainly gave him a scrap! *Abruptly excited and cunning:* Georgie, I'll tell you! That two weeks' clause—they can give me notice any time, but *I* can give *them* notice, too!

Georgie looks questioning.

FRANK: Don't you see? They can let me out, but *I* can walk out any time I want! If I feel I'm breaking my neck—

GEORGIE: You can quit?

FRANK: Yeah, that's sort of what I mean, yeah. *Bright and shrewd:* You see? Get it?

GEORGIE, *dubious and waiting:* Yes . . .

FRANK, *cunningly grand:* Why, with this two weeks' clause I don't even have to come into New York, do I?

Georgie murmurs a "No" as Frank seats himself, chortling.

FRANK: That's the thing, that's it—two can play the same game! *Delighted at this discovery, Georgie much less so, Frank abruptly snaps his fingers and lights up even more.* Wait a minute! Quarter to seven this morning I had a dream! I laughed so hard it woke me up! That's a sign, Georgie, a hunch!

GEORGIE, *puzzled:* A dream?

FRANK, *seeing it:* A big sign—now get this—a big banner was stretched across the street: "Frank Elgin in . . ." I couldn't make out in what. Mayor La Guardia was in the dream—lots of people laughing and feeling good. I'm going to take that part, Georgie! You don't have to tell me not to drink—haven't I been a good boy all summer? *He moves around.* This morning I got up early—that funny laughing dream. And I was thinking about our lives—everything—and now this chance! Don't you see that all those people in the dream, they wish me luck. I won't fail this time! Because that's what counts—if the world is with you—and your wife! *He looks at her, earnest, boyish, and questioning, appealing for her support.*

GEORGIE, *finally, with reluctance:* I don't have any appointments . . . all winter . . .

FRANK, *excitedly:* That's what counts! I can't fail this time— I feel like Jack-a-Million! I'll let Dodd know—I'll go up to the office in person. *He takes the twenty-dollar bill.* But my first stop is the barbershop—I want the tonsorial works. Anything you want me to bring *you* back?

GEORGIE: No . . .

FRANK: Catch that, dear!

He throws her an extravagant kiss, really excited, and she catches the gift with an open hand. Alone, thinking, we see

how unhappy Georgie is. Then she remembers her suitcase;
she takes it from under the bed, opens it, and unhappily looks
down at its contents. Then, murmuring, "My God, my God,
my God . . ." she takes out a dress, goes back to the wardrobe,
and replaces it on a hanger.

Curtain

ACT ONE: *Scene 3*

≫≫-≫≫-≫≫-≫≫-≫≫-≫≫-≫≫-≫≫-≫≫-≫≫-≫≫-≫≫≪≪-≪≪-≪≪-≪≪-≪≪-≪≪-≪≪-≪≪-≪≪-≪≪-≪≪-≪≪

The rehearsal stage, ten days later. Bernie, his back to the audience, is sitting to one side, watching Frank and Nancy play a scene. Larry, at the work table, is the only other person in the theater. It is late at night and the outer world has stopped for these working people; they have the quality of functioning fully, unaware of anything else.

Nancy is seventeen and virginal, which is to say untried and initiatory; but she has real if unfocused talent. Frank is working well, old muscles slowly coming to life; but he is worried about an inability to memorize his lines, although he will not say so. His part is rolled up in his hand. Nancy is letter perfect.

FRANK, *in the play, with an Irish flavor:* "You know me, Ellen. You call me granddad, but I'm all your parents rolled into one. Consequently I have to talk to you as father and mother too. Now why do you like that boy?"

NANCY: "I don't know. Maybe because he likes me."

FRANK: "That's a human enough reason. How long do you know the lad?"

BERNIE: Play him suspicious, Frank, suspicious—you don't trust her!

FRANK: "No, you told me—four months. That ain't very long, as time goes, is it?"

NANCY: "Why, four months can be eternity, Granddad! Didn't you know that?"

37

FRANK: "I guess I knew it, Ellen, but forgot it." *Pause.* "Now, what about that boy?"

NANCY: "Oh, you mustn't worry about him—he's only one of a dozen! I'm very popular, you know."

FRANK, *after a pause:* That's me! Throw me the line, Larry.

LARRY: "Yes, you're a grown-up lady now . . ."

FRANK, *back in the play:* "Yes, you're a grown-up lady now . . ." *He stops again.* Now what?

NANCY, *answering automatically, before Larry can:* "But I can easily call to mind when you were this high."

LARRY: That's right.

FRANK, *stops and looks grumpily at Nancy:* Never usurp the stage manager's position, dear. Older actors don't like it.

NANCY, *overwhelmed:* I beg your pardon—I'm very sorry, Mr. Elgin.

BERNIE, *impatiently:* Let's go, let's go . . .

FRANK, *resumes the play, a headache building up in him:* "But I can easily call to mind when you were . . . this high. You had a funny habit. You said when you'd grow big I'd grow small. Children have that delusion, don't they?" *He turns.* That's tricky there, Bernie, a real mouthful.

BERNIE: That's true.

FRANK, *hesitating:* What does he mean?

BERNIE, *moving in:* First, a real psychological fact about kids. But the theatrical meaning is more important. Show that he's trying to win her over to his side.

FRANK: But he isn't the kind who would *openly* ask for sympathy.

BERNIE: Normally, no, but this is his only grandchild—his defenses are down.

Frank thinks about this somberly.

NANCY, *timidly:* Do *I* know that he wants sympathy?

BERNIE, *looking at his watch:* No, Ellen doesn't understand the situation yet. Wow, it's almost eleven o'clock!

LARRY, *with typical tact and deference:* I was just about to call your attention to that.

BERNIE: Tell you what—let's send Nancy home. Our little ingénue needs her beauty rest.

NANCY, *earnestly:* I'm not tired at all, truly I'm not!

BERNIE: Don't rush, child—life is long.

The scene breaks up with the quality of a seventh-inning stretch.

NANCY: Well, will you want me at ten tomorrow then?

BERNIE, *ogling her:* Why?

NANCY, *flustered:* Well, I mean I'm available whenever you want me, night or day. *The men laugh.* Oh, I didn't mean *that!* I can't bear it! I mean I wanted to get my hair washed tomorrow and—

BERNIE, *grinning:* All right, come in at eleven. And beat a hasty retreat right now, before I forget I'm a parent myself! I eat little girls like you, without salt!

LARRY: Button up your coat and don't look so flustered—we all adore you.

NANCY, *simpering:* You're very nasty, all of you, tonight! *Laughing:* Good night, everyone. Happy dreams!

ALL: Good night, good night.

Nancy goes out, happy and self-conscious, full of young excitement.

FRANK: Off in a flurry of tender jingle bells—that's the age.

LARRY: Baby.

BERNIE: Larryola, you don't have to hang around.

LARRY: Want me to put out the pilot light?

Abstracted, leafing through his script, Bernie murmurs, "Yeah, sure . . ." Larry drags out the pilot light and shuts off a strip of border lights while Frank sits at Bernie's table. The feeling of the scene, out of which the above joshing came, is late and tired.

FRANK: Did I hear you say you were a parent?

BERNIE: I have a little girl of four.

FRANK: There's nothing quite like a little girl. Funny, I never got the impression you were married.

BERNIE: Neither did my wife. Five months ago she invented a phrase, "The Perennial Bachelor," and went to Reno to patent the invention! *Of the script:* What about this damn hospital scene? You tired? *He yawns.* Wanna stop?

FRANK: Well, I have a touch of headache—

BERNIE: Let's stop—

FRANK, *troubled:* No, let's go on. Judge Murray's character escapes me.

BERNIE: Well, let's chase him.

FRANK: Who's he like in real life? Hague, Hines . . . ?

BERNIE: Any of those big political bosses. *He turns to Larry, who is leaving.* What's tomorrow morning's call?

LARRY: Whole company at eleven. Except Mabel Beck—she's got that radio shot.

BERNIE: Scan the horizon, Larry. Come back if that little man is still outside.

Larry nods sympathetically and goes. Bernie pauses pensively.

BERNIE: In my old age I'm ducking a man with a summons. Money—my wife wants money.

FRANK, *sympathetically:* Oh, no . . .

Real loneliness shows itself in Bernie, but he briskly pulls himself together.

BERNIE, *crossing to Frank:* Let's talk about the character. How do *you* feel the Judge?

FRANK: Can I go wild? *Then intently, seeing and feeling something inwardly:* A fox—that's the image. Nimble. Quiet. On the alert, but nothing shows—a rigid face. A concrete slab for a face . . .

BERNIE: That's power . . .

FRANK: That's power—and pride.

BERNIE: Pride's a big color to work for.

FRANK: Yes, he can't be wrong. Got everything he wants. Above the battle—withdrawn.

His face narrow with thought, Frank has begun to illustrate his words; a ridiculous and cagey strut comes into his walk.

FRANK, *murmuring, in the role:* I'm illiterate—why?

BERNIE: Because he's narrow, prejudiced, intolerant—

FRANK: But that's his strength.

BERNIE, *agreeing:* That's his strength—he goes narrow but deep—his own man.

FRANK, *excitedly, staying in the mask:* I can do that—sure! Now I know how this boy-o walks and talks! That's in his way . . .

Without a change of expression, Frank sends a chair scuttling across the stage with one powerful vicious kick. Imperturbably he struts back to Bernie and drops back to himself.

FRANK: Isn't that it?

BERNIE, *admiringly:* That's it.

FRANK, *eagerly:* But I have to like him, Bernie, even when he puts his wife away. Otherwise I can't get inside him.

BERNIE, *admiringly:* Where do you get these kind of feelings from?

FRANK: I don't know . . . *He circles a hand around his chest.* But when I get it here, inside—you can't get it technically.

BERNIE: No, you're not a technical actor.

FRANK, *sighing:* Not many directors understood that about me.

BERNIE: Smoke?

Silence. Moodiness. Both men light up and smoke cigarettes while putting on their coats. Frank looks at his part.

FRANK: I'm worried about the lines . . .

BERNIE: Don't answer if you don't want to—how did a man with your talents go so haywire?

FRANK, *evasively:* That's a bow-wow with a very long tail.

BERNIE: What kind of woman is your wife? Just for chatter's sake . . .

FRANK: Georgie's got a very good mind.

BERNIE: Then why didn't she want you to play this part?

FRANK: Was that your impression?

BERNIE: A yard wide!

FRANK, *evasively:* I don't know—she's on a hairspring, Georgie. Always has been—a hairspring. *He leafs nervously through his part.* Sorry I don't know the words yet, Bernie. I wanted to surprise you tonight, but non compos mentis.

BERNIE: The sooner you get that second act out of your hands, the better. Why on a hairspring?

FRANK, *uneasily:* It's like the hospital scene in the play. Where they tell the Judge his wife is—psychotic? What's the exact meaning of the word?

BERNIE: Insane . . .

FRANK, *looking at his part, his voice low:* The Judge, you see . . . isn't glad to get rid of his wife, the way the author says. It's very complicated. *He clears his throat.* You tell an unhappily married man his wife is insane. He may feel relief, but at the same time he hopes it isn't true.

BERNIE, *watching him keenly:* That makes a richer scene.

FRANK: You can even say it's tender when he gets the news. There's so much to remember of living together—all the winters and summers, the times they were poor . . . *His voice trembles.* And the fights, snarling and yipping—settling blue murder with an hour in the bed . . .

BERNIE, *keenly:* Yes, if you played the scene that way . . .

FRANK: I'm not talking about the scene.

BERNIE: You're not?

FRANK, *fingering his part:* Georgie . . . was "Miss America" in the late '30s, the year I met her. She gave up a big career to marry me.

BERNIE, *delicately:* Is that according to Luke or Mark? You or her?

FRANK, *turning:* Don't you believe me?

BERNIE: Sure, but what the hell is "Miss America" past twenty-five or thirty? What career? Marriage doesn't suit women any more—they don't want a home: the only piece of furniture they'll touch is the psychoanalyst's couch!

FRANK, *solemnly:* It cost me thousands . . .

BERNIE, *bitterly:* I had it for five years with the former Mrs. Dodd.

FRANK: I bought a fourteen-room house down in Great Neck the year we married. Never knew a better life. Swimming, boating, tennis, dinner at six—at seven she'd kiss me good-by and I'd drive into town for my show. On matinee days she'd come in and we'd stay out late. Little spats and things, but it looked like a dream life to me. And then one night, from way out left field—don't know what hit me—I find her dead drunk across a bed—a kid who never took a real drink in her life! I didn't catch on that year—who could figure *that?* Career versus career—she didn't want me to play! Bernie, she was a hopeless drunkard inside a year. Then we had a child . . . *Moved, he pauses.* After that . . . every part I play, it's just like I ran off with another woman. I begin to drink myself. Don't ask me where the money went. She cuts her wrists, sets fire to a hotel suite—any time I'm on the stage she needs a nurse to watch her. And then, finally, we lost the child. You don't say, "Go to hell, good-by!" do you? By 1940, '41—well, when you're in that situation you beat a bottle hard!

There is a hushed pause. Bernie pulls at an ear.

BERNIE: Does she still drink?

FRANK, *smiling ruefully and standing:* She stopped when I began. But I know how to handle her now—backwards, like a crab. About this part—to give you an instance—I had to make believe I didn't want this part. That leaves it open for *her* to convince me, her idea, not mine, see?

Both men are standing. Bernie, with a soft exclamation, gathers up his things on the table.

BERNIE: I guess you have to bring her up to Boston. I'm not against it. *My* wife was so twisted, "I hope your next play's a big flop!" she says. "So the whole world can see I love you even if you're a failure!" *He turns.* As far as the work's concerned, I'm very pleased.

FRANK, *eagerly:* You are?

BERNIE: You're a born actor, Frank, and this can mean the world to you.

FRANK, *solemnly:* I appreciate it, son.

BERNIE, *grinning:* And don't call me son again—I don't like it. *As they are about to leave:* Can your wife louse you up in this show?

FRANK: Don't worry, I can handle her. You know, you're a hot, gifted guy who got somewhere in a hurry. But you might be surprised in another ten years what you'll do for a little companionship.

BERNIE, *flatly:* No one now living, under or over the earth, will ever again put me out on a tether! I go wild when— *He stops abruptly, looking over Frank's shoulder.*

Frank turns around. Georgie has just entered. From her reserved but pleasant manner neither man can tell what she has heard.

FRANK, *quickly:* Georgie, what are you doing here? Where you coming from?

GEORGIE: From the movie show. Passing by. I thought you might be through.

FRANK: We were just breaking up.

BERNIE, *quietly:* Your timing was perfect—good evening, Mrs. Elgin.

GEORGIE, *smiling:* Yes, I have a knack that way. Good evening, Mr. Dodd. How is my husband doing?

BERNIE: In my less than humble opinion, he's what they call a natural.

GEORGIE: Did I intrude?

FRANK *and* BERNIE, *together:* Not at all, we were going to—
No, we were just closing—

GEORGIE: I don't like to make myself obtrusive when Frank is working. Unless he needs my help, of course. Am I in the way?

BERNIE, *taking her measure:* No, we were just closing up shop and giving it back to the theater ghosts.

Smiling vaguely, Georgie steps down to the footlights and looks out at the house. She stands there, unconscious of a kind of oriental posturing, consisting of a listening attitude and a faint smile both polite and deprecating; she is her own aristocratic personage, unaware that a certain air of breeding never leaves her.

GEORGIE, *softly:* Nothing is quite so mysterious and silent as a dark theater . . . a night without a star . . .

Frank and Bernie look at each other.

BERNIE: Why don't we go out for some coffee?

FRANK: Georgie? She makes all the decisions in our family.

BERNIE, *very politely:* Is that true, Mrs. Elgin?

GEORGIE, *archly:* To the extent that Frank's brought out the mother in me, yes. I'd like some coffee. And I'd like to get to know Mr. Dodd better.

BERNIE: And I'd like to get to know you better.

GEORGIE, *looking out again:* The theater is mysterious . . .

BERNIE: That's true . . .

She smiles at him and goes off right, followed by Frank. Bernie, looking reflectively after them, drops his cigarette, steps on it, and starts off.

Slow Curtain

ACT ONE: *Scene 4*

>>>->>>->>>->>>->>>->>>->>>->>>->>>->>>->>>->)<<<-<<<-<<<-<<<-<<<-<<<-<<<-<<<-<<<-<<<-<<<-<<<

Frank's room, as before, a week later. It is early morning. The bed is disarranged. Frank, suspenders hanging, is finishing shaving. Ebullient, in rare form, he keeps dressing throughout the scene. Georgie, wearing a wrapper, is pouring coffee at a little folding table, downstage left.

FRANK: Gonna get me some real expensive shaving lotion any minute now! Little things like that . . . the spice of life.

GEORGIE: What?

FRANK, *raising his voice:* Shaving lotion, toots; I want some luxuries out of life!

GEORGIE: You talk like a courtesan, Frank.

FRANK: Then put me smack-dab in the middle of the courtesans if they like luxuries, too! Boy-o, I'll be glad to get away from this Chinese laundry! *He shakes out a shirt.* The way they do shirts—it's a crime and a shame! Look at this! And they don't even give away free nuts any more!

GEORGIE, *who is very nearsighted:* Let's see, where would I be if I were a pair of glasses?

FRANK: Right in my paws! *He picks up the glasses and hands them to her. Chortling:* See? You couldn't get along without me, Georgiana!

49

GEORGIE, *smiling:* Someone's feeling mighty good today. *She stops, having kicked over two empty beer bottles on the floor. She looks up seriously at Frank.*

FRANK, *appealingly:* Put down that tomahawk. Didn't hide them, did I? Those two bottles of beer gave me a good night's sleep.

GEORGIE: When did you get them?

FRANK: After you fell asleep. I walked to the corner—got a *News* and a *Mirror,* the *Tribune* for you.

She looks at him thoughtfully, but he refuses to take her seriously.

FRANK: Now, come on, Georgie, have a heart: I didn't hide the bottles and I got a good night's sleep.

GEORGIE: Are you worried about anything?

FRANK, *readily, with a broad Italian accent:* Nothing is a-worry me, except-a the lines. Poppa Hubbard, he's a-go to the cupboard and is a-bare!

GEORGIE, *quietly:* Don't start drinking beer, Frank. I'll get you some sleeping pills today. One a night can't hurt.

She sips coffee as he goes to the mirror to tie his tie.

FRANK: Gosh, I'm getting baggy under the eyes. Sometimes I ask myself if it's me. *Into the mirror:* Hey, is that you, Frank? *A basso profundo answer:* Yesss. *Then:* Need a few ties, too, don't I?

GEORGIE: Wouldn't know where to start, you need so many things. Wait and see what happens.

FRANK: Yeah, we'll soon know—oh, those critics! Mamma mia, those critics!

GEORGIE, *sipping coffee:* How are they up in Boston?

FRANK: Leave it to Poppa—he can charm a bird off a branch. No, ma'am, I'm not worried—not a thing. I'm taking it all in my stride! *He throws a towel aside and goes to the table.* Oh, my, when I think of those great big fluffy bath towels in a good hotel! We're gonna have fun, baby—you know that, don't you? Wait'll I lock you in that hotel room!

GEORGIE: Drink your coffee, Rooster.

FRANK: Yes, sir, everything is good and solid! It's autumn again—I'm rehearsing a show—hear that? Let the wind blow down the street—the oysters and lobsters are delicious! *Of the coffee:* Hey, that's been near the fire!

GEORGIE: Look before you leap, silly.

FRANK, *grimacing:* My tie straight?

GEORGIE: Straight. Your shoes are being soled and heeled, the black ones. What else?

FRANK, *sitting, appealingly:* Blow on Frank's coffee for him?

She smiles. He sips the coffee carefully, looking at his paper.

FRANK: Who could dream it—to blow a double-header! How do you like it—I'll miss the whole series up in Boston!

GEORGIE, *after a pause:* Frank, does Bernie Dodd like me?

FRANK, *overcasually careful:* Why shouldn't the boy like you?

GEORGIE, *sincerely:* I don't know. Seems to be a chip on his shoulder. Does he like women?

FRANK, *innocently:* He's been married, divorced, has a child . . .

GEORGIE: I don't mind him not liking me, but shouldn't we face it realistically if it's true?

FRANK, *lightly:* See how it goes? Leave you alone for a few days and you get morbid.

GEORGIE, *patiently quiet:* Seriously, for your own sake, Frank. There's too much at stake. I don't want to be in your way.

FRANK, *abruptly, with edge:* Georgie, I'm winging like a lark —a million bucks couldn't compensate for this feeling of being back in harness!

GEORGIE, *agreeing:* I haven't seen you with such zip in ten years.

FRANK: Then why make trouble, dear? When we get up to Boston I'm going—

GEORGIE, *quietly:* I'm not going up to Boston. My fine, womanly intuition tells me that Mr. Dodd doesn't want me there.

FRANK, *angrily:* Yes, but *I* want you up in Boston! *He moves around.* That's all I need in this day and age—to leave my wife alone here, in a city full of wolves!

GEORGIE, *soberly:* Are you jealous?

FRANK: What the hell are you talking about? Would I take this job without you? I *need* you up in Boston!

GEORGIE, *simply:* If you need me up in Boston—that's most likely where I'll be. *She stops him from saying anything.* That's enough, Frank—we've said enough. *She crosses.* You'll be late. *Smiling:* You have a real conviction of woman's perfidy, don't you?

FRANK, *sullenly:* I thought we'd said enough.

Georgie has gone to the wardrobe for his suit coat; she brings it down, beckons him over, and holds it for him.

GEORGIE: I haven't felt like a woman in ten years.

FRANK, *still sullen:* I suppose that's my fault.

GEORGIE, *lightly:* Summer dies, autumn comes, a fact of nature—nobody's fault.

FRANK: Didn't you sew on this loose button?

She crosses to a drawer for needle and thread, looking back archly.

GEORGIE: Spoiling for a fight, aren't you?

He refuses to answer. She sits and, sewing on the button deftly, speaks with serious lightness.

GEORGIE: You mystify me, Frank, your sense of guilt and insecurity. Take a lesson from my father, the late Delaney the Great. He didn't care what people thought of him, no matter what he did. Played every vaudeville house in the world. Didn't show up at home but twice a year—and those two times he was down in the cellar perfecting new magic tricks.

FRANK: Oh, sure, you'd love that—seeing me only twice a year!

GEORGIE, *whimsically:* My mother didn't mind it as much as I did—it orphaned me. Might not have married you if I'd had a father. But he *believed* in himself, I mean—you don't. That's cost you plenty . . . it's cost me as much . . .

She bites off the thread and holds up the coat for him again. Simmering, he slips into it.

FRANK: You want me to beg you, don't you?

GEORGIE, *puzzled:* Beg me what?

FRANK: To come up to Boston.

GEORGIE: I thought we'd settled that. *Disgruntled, he is looking at the coat.* I pressed it last night.

FRANK: Where's that lousy part?

GEORGIE: In your right-hand pocket.

FRANK, *feeling sheepish, laughing a little, brings out the part and a small address book:* See, you can't live without me. But I don't know why you talk that way—winter, summer—you're still a kid.

GEORGIE, *with a moue:* Oh, sure, of course, why not.

FRANK, *holds up the address book, needling her:* Well, it's a small world. Took her address—she's living up in Boston now. Susie Lewis from Saratoga Springs. Our playwright's aunt, no less! He brought her around last night. Haven't seen her in eighteen years!

GEORGIE: Attractive?

FRANK: Widowed and sitting on a mint.

GEORGIE, *smiling, putting a handkerchief in his upper pocket:* I'd investigate if I were you.

FRANK: Sue? She'd have me in a minute! *Then, all dressed:* Well, am I decent?

GEORGIE, *nodding:* Say good morning to Bernardo the Great for me.

FRANK, *getting his topcoat:* You can bet your sweet Fanny Maloney I won't tell him what you're calling him! Don't you go tangling with him at the run-through tomorrow night!

GEORGIE, *stops him at the door by asking:* Run-through?

FRANK, *caught:* Now, don't tell me I didn't tell you about it. I didn't tell you yesterday?

GEORGIE: Maybe you told Susie Peppermint or whatever her name is. Don't you want me to come tomorrow night? *She is slightly irked by his hesitant manner.* Oh, come on, Frank, tell me what you want me to do. I won't love you less.

FRANK, *uneasily:* Don't feel offended, dear. I'd feel better if you didn't come. This isn't a dress rehearsal—just a run-through with a few props. *Wryly:* They want the backers to see what they're getting for their dough.

GEORGIE, *easily:* Then I'll see it in Boston with the sets and the costumes.

FRANK, *fondly:* 'At's my girl! *He starts out.* My only real worry is the lines—they won't stick in the dome!

GEORGIE: We'll drill some more—I'll cue you. Frank, don't get secretive. If I go on the road with you, tell me straight out anything that's on your mind. Don't shuffle—I don't often talk this way any more. We're both of us miles behind. Don't try to catch up all at once. We both know what's happened in the past. We'll have to live one day at a time, without resentments and evasions. We're at the bottom—

FRANK, *stoutly:* But we'll be at the top!

GEORGIE, *correcting him:* But one rung at a time, separated by quiet, healthy sleep.

FRANK, *squirming:* Yeah, you're right, dear, you're right.

GEORGIE: He's young, but he's a good man, that Dodd. Talk out all your worries with him. *She looks at him keenly.*

FRANK, *lowering his gaze:* I love you, Georgie. *He goes to the door and turns, about to throw her a defiant kiss.* Catch this one—it's a lulu! No, really get it.

He returns, holds and kisses her, then turns and goes. She smiles faintly to herself. After a moment she goes to the table and, whistling softly to herself, takes some of the coffee things to the sink. Returning, the rhythm of her whistling slows down as she sees the beer bottles. She picks them up, looks at them with a thought; then she places them under the sink. She whistles again as she starts for the little table once more.

Curtain

ACT ONE: *Scene 5*

>>>->>>->>>->>>->>>->>>->>>->>>->>>->>>->>>-><<<-<<<-<<<-<<<-<<<-<<<-<<<-<<<-<<<-<<<-<<<-<<

Frank's dressing room in a Boston theater a week later, around midnight. There is a wide make-up shelf on the right wall, a mirror above it, a chair in front of it. Against the back wall is a couch. Downstage left are a pier glass and a chest of drawers. On top of the chest is a small radio. The door is at the left, upstage of these.

A first dress rehearsal has just been concluded onstage. A murmur of voices is heard outside the door of the empty, untidy room. Larry, the stage manager, looks in; seeing no one, he is about to leave, changes his mind, and heads for the make-up shelf, where he helps himself impatiently to a cigarette and a match. A fretful Unger looks in, a script under one arm.

UNGER: Frank? Where's Frank?

LARRY: Looking for him myself.

The two men meet in the middle of the room.

UNGER: I have a few more cuts in Scene Four.

LARRY: I'll take them later, if you don't mind. I'm trying to find out what happened in Scene Six. They keep blowing in the same spot.

UNGER, *as they go out:* Six? I think the girl's throwing the wrong cue. Watch her when she walks down to the table.

LARRY: I don't know—maybe. Frank cuts in there a moment too soon and . . .

57

The stage is empty again; outside the voices of stagehands are heard. A moment later Georgie enters, surprised to find the room empty. She is chewing gum and wearing glasses. She wipes her nose with a tissue, then begins to tidy up, chiefly picking up garments and brushing a coat. Bernie enters.

BERNIE: Where's Frank?

GEORGIE: Isn't he onstage?

BERNIE: No. *He sniffs.* Cobra?

GEORGIE, *smiling:* Wisteria.

BERNIE, *about to exit, returns:* Keeping in mind that it was a damn rough first dress rehearsal—the first time they've played in the sets—what did you think of the show?

GEORGIE: Oh, I didn't judge—just sat and listened to the words. But Frank looks wonderful, doesn't he? *She removes her chewing gum.* Chewed the flavor out of this two hours ago.

Each is trying to get on a good footing with the other. Bernie lights a cigarette.

BERNIE: Smoke?

GEORGIE: Never use them.

BERNIE: There's a whole pack since eight o'clock. These are really bad ones, these dress rehearsal nights. Knock on wood—not one real case of nerves yet. The show's new to you, isn't it? What did you think of friend Frank?

GEORGIE: He was very tense, poor chick.

Bernie crosses to the make-up shelf, throws away the crumpled cigarette pack.

GEORGIE: I'm fairly level-headed, making allowances for my sex, but I'd be in a blizzard, too, if my show were this ragged just before opening night.

BERNIE: But that's what two more dress rehearsals are for.

GEORGIE: You're as tense as a bug in June, aren't you?

BERNIE, *laughing:* Shh—not so loud. My cast thinks I'm made of steel. Everyone looks for Poppa on an opening week and I'm it.

GEORGIE: Frank thinks the sun rises and sets in you, Mr. Dodd.

BERNIE, *carefully:* You'd make me very happy by being careful with Frank. You're his wife—he's probably all focused on your reaction.

GEORGIE: Is his performance pleasing you?

BERNIE: What do *you* think?

GEORGIE: Don't ask me. I had one long old-fashioned cry out there. Just a country girl. *She sits, having hung up all of Frank's clothes.*

BERNIE: Give him another week or two. He'll be very good.

GEORGIE, *thinking:* But the show opens Wednesday night.

BERNIE, *reassuringly:* They'll get a show up here, but not what they'll get in New York.

GEORGIE: But what about Frank's notices here, on Thursday morning? You can't tell the Boston critics he'll be wonderful in *New York.*

BERNIE: That's the chance we take. Out-of-town tryouts mean education in public. You think Frank's that bad?

GEORGIE: I think he's wonderful! *Hesitantly:* But I do wish I could follow the shape of what he's doing.

BERNIE: Too much detail, you mean?

GEORGIE, *carefully:* Yes, since you put it that way.

BERNIE, *crosses abruptly to her and speaks with a consciously used air of candor, like a politician:* I think I can trust your intelligence, Mrs. Elgin. Most actors don't need four weeks' rehearsing. They repeat the same glib, superficial patterns they found the first or second week. The usual actor gives himself small aims—or the director does it for him. In a couple of weeks they're fulfilled. And it all fits into a small, dull peanut shell.

GEORGIE: And you think Frank—?

BERNIE, *humorously:* No peanut shell, he. His talent—the quality of it is improvisatory. That's his blessing and his burden—he never knows what he is going to do next.

GEORGIE, *thoughtfully:* That's very keen of you to notice that. Many of his personal problems come from that.

BERNIE: He explores and discovers, as an actor, opening up the part very slowly. And my problem is to keep him going— overflowing. The longer I keep him fluid and open, the more gold we mine.

GEORGIE: You shut his talent off if you rein him in?

BERNIE, *nodding:* That's why I want him fluid for another week or two. Let him flounder—in *his* case it's healthy. New York's five long weeks away. *He goes to the door.* Don't mention any of this to Frank.

GEORGIE, *stoutly:* I won't be that foolish, Mr. Dodd.

BERNIE: I know you won't. Tell him I'll be right back.

He looks at her carefully, with a polite charm masking a certain scorn, then leaves. Despite her awareness of his good sense, Georgie is somewhat disturbed by him. Thinking, she turns on a small radio. She looks up as Frank enters. He begins undressing, but his attitude is questioning. Frank is an imposing and somewhat romantic figure, in evening clothes, a portly political boss with gray hair and mustache. Nervous and tired, he slams his part down on the make-up shelf.

FRANK: I was upstairs, running lines with the kid. I blew like a bat all night. I hope this doesn't happen Wednesday, when we open. Well, what's the verdict?

She looks at him, very moved, momentarily not knowing how to grapple with his mood. He is afraid to hear what she will say.

GEORGIE: Frank, you look wonderful. I scarcely recognized you out there.

FRANK: Was it bad?

GEORGIE, *gently:* Nothing was bad, dear. It was a bad rehearsal, of course.

FRANK, *disapppointed and glum:* Yeah, I floundered like a fish, didn't I? What else did you see? I won't faint—you can tell me if I'm bad!

GEORGIE, *quietly:* I think you'll be astonishing in the part.

FRANK: Maybe my eye is jaundiced—you don't look astonished to me!

GEORGIE: Maybe I'm a little choked up, Frank.

Frank looks at her with suspicion, not trusting her. Irritably he throws his collar against the mirror.

GEORGIE: You're keyed up and nervous. Be as unreasonable as you like.

FRANK, *outraged:* Didn't you just see me act for the first time in seven years? Say hello, good-by, or kiss my foot! But don't stand there like Minne-ha-ha! *Sulking, Frank pulls off his shirt and begins removing a stomach padding.*

GEORGIE, *hanging up his coat, trying to josh him out of his mood:* I *thought* you were a little thick in the middle . . .

FRANK, *muttering:* I need the portliness. If I ever learn these lines, I'll call it Columbus Day! *He cocks another suspicious eye at her, lights a cigarette, puts on a robe, and sits at the make-up shelf. He begins removing his make-up.*

GEORGIE: Frank, I don't . . . YOU'RE MAGNIFICENT IN THIS PART! And the play—I'm deeply surprised that quiet, smiling boy has so much talent!

FRANK: Shut the radio off!

She crosses and does so. He sniffs loudly, blows his nose, and clears his throat.

GEORGIE: Are you catching a cold?

FRANK, *morosely:* That's all I need this week—a cold! I'd be a dead bunny for sure! You need more than a haircut to play this part—that's what *I* know!

GEORGIE, *crosses and offers him aspirins:* Aspirins?

FRANK, *rejecting them testily:* Give me a minute, dear! *He has bent down and is about to unlace his shoes in the same hurried rhythm which has blown him into the room; he stops abruptly, dropping his foot to the floor.*

GEORGIE: What's the matter?

FRANK: Look at me going—zip, zip, zip! I can't even catch my breath! Why don't they get me a dresser? Don't I deserve it? How can I make those fast changes by myself?

GEORGIE: Do you want me to speak to Mr. Cook about it?

FRANK, *not looking at her:* Speak to Cook about it. Cook or Bernie. They can afford it with the salary I'm getting. *He turns abruptly.* Do you know Mabel Beck gets more than I do? Five hundred a week—and she stinks up every scene!

GEORGIE, *quietly:* She isn't bad in the part.

FRANK: That's right—stand up for everybody else! And look at that Nancy kid! Don't they learn stage deportment any more? Upstaged me twice tonight! *He acts it out.* Once I didn't even know where in the hell she was! *He begins to clean up.*

GEORGIE, *laughing soothingly:* Now, Frank, come on, take it easy. You'll have yourself believing all this nonsense before the week's out. First things first. Work well—that's your only concern.

FRANK, *promptly:* How'm I supposed to work with that damn understudy snooping around in the wings? Is that nonsense too?

GEORGIE: Speak to Mr. Dodd about it.

FRANK: *You* speak to him about it. Tell him to keep the guy out front.

GEORGIE: What're you looking for? Aspirins? They're right under your nose.

FRANK: Yeah, but where's my nose?

He laughs sheepishly, ashamed of his bad humor. This breaks the tension between them. While he is swallowing aspirins

and water, a knock sounds at the door. Frank calls "Come!"
Unger enters with Cook behind him. Frank's manner changes
immediately. A jovial, self-deprecating humor is his protective
mask. Nothing seems to bother him.

FRANK: Welcome, gentry! Don't tell me about the show! I
know—stank on rye bread!

UNGER, *sincerely:* Not to me. That hospital scene put a fine
prickle on my skin.

FRANK, *pleased:* Don't kid the ugly man! Hear that, Georgie?
The boy must like me.

UNGER: I like a good actor.

COOK, *gloomily sitting, to say something:* Me, too.

BERNIE, *coming in jauntily at the door:* Why's everyone so
depressed?

FRANK, *gaily:* Not me, I'm not depressed.

UNGER: Neither am I. I think the show's in swell shape.

COOK: Me, too, but it wasn't a very good dress rehearsal, was
it?

BERNIE, *laughing heartily:* The worst damn dress rehearsal
I've ever seen!

COOK: Then I fail to see the humor. I may be dense. Am I
dense?

UNGER: I, if I may be excused, I have a date with my typewriter and a pocketful of notes.

BERNIE: Call you in the morning, Paul.

UNGER, *going:* Fine. Good night, all you keepers of my integ-
rity.

FRANK: Nice boy, one in a million. Not a speck of ego in him.

LARRY, *after tapping discreetly at the open door:* Excuse me, Frank. I have all the last scene people onstage. I'd like to run the spot where everyone blew—we can't locate what happened.

FRANK, *protestingly:* But I just ran it with the kid.

LARRY, *politely:* I'd be very obliged, Frank, if you'd run it again for me and the rest of the cast?

FRANK, *gets up with a mock groan, excutes a half-dance step:* Oi, gentry, oi! Duty calls, but I'll be back. *Towel in hand, he goes with Larry.*

BERNIE: *Frank's* in high, good humor.

GEORGIE, *quietly:* Yes, he is.

COOK, *glumly:* Me, too, but don't ask me why. If he spoke one line of the author's script tonight, it never reached my ears.

BERNIE: Cookie, why do they open shows out of town?

COOK: Bernie, I'll never know. Will he know his lines for opening night?

BERNIE, *annoyed:* A little gray matter, Phil. He tripped on a rug he'd never seen before tonight! He couldn't find his slippers. His specs were in a drawer that wouldn't open, and a dozen other things! What do you want, miracles? Of course he dropped his lines!

COOK: I'm not worried. Like the author—me, too—I beg to be excused. The crew is still out there on double time.

GEORGIE, *stops him as he sulkily starts for the door:* Mr. Cook, do you think Frank needs a dresser?

COOK, *holding back his exasperation:* No, I don't. But I suppose you do?

BERNIE, *helping her:* What does Frank think?

GEORGIE: Those two quick changes—it's a very large part, after all . . .

Bernie makes a signal of assent behind Georgie's back.

COOK: I know, Bernie—you think I eat shredded fifty-dollar bills for salad. *He shakes his head dolefully and walks out.*

BERNIE: Don't worry, we'll get him a dresser.

GEORGIE: Mr. Cook is almost what the bad fairy promised Frank at his cradle.

BERNIE: He's not that bad.

GEORGIE: I'm glad *we're* getting along, Mr. Dodd.

BERNIE, *archly:* Did you think we wouldn't?

GEORGIE: You smoke too much. *Then:* Who is that tall, gloomy man that lurks around backstage? Lucas? Is that the name?

BERNIE, *agreeable but wary:* Yes. General understudy. Not much personality but competent.

GEORGIE: Excuse me for saying this—must he stay backstage? It seems to bother Frank.

BERNIE: I'll watch that. But is Frank that insecure? He's working well, in good humor all the time—

GEORGIE, *with a friendly laugh:* Golly, don't you know he hides behind that humor? He's not a simple man, Mr. Dodd. That's why I offer myself as a sort of liaison officer between you both.

BERNIE: Is that what you're doing?

GEORGIE, *breaking:* I hope you don't misunderstand—

BERNIE: No, I think I understand.

GEORGIE: Certain kinds of men, you know, are very strange. Business couldn't be better, wife and kiddies are fine. The next day you read he's hung himself from the chandelier. He can be the biggest kidder too—it doesn't matter.

BERNIE, *solemnly:* Is that a picture of Frank?

GEORGIE, *carefully, a little afraid:* Yes and no. He doesn't like to make the slightest remark that might lose him people's regard or affection. I've simply grown into the habit of doing it for him.

Bernie pauses, looking at her with a polite, regretful air.

BERNIE: I'm really sorry to say so, Mrs. Elgin, but I hired an actor, a *good* actor. I may want him without his sisters and his cousins and his aunts.

Georgie, withdrawn, doesn't know what to say to this. Bernie, watching and testing her, sits.

BERNIE: What, for instance, bothers him now?

GEORGIE, *pausing, then plunging:* Mr. Cook. His attitude. The ever-present understudy. The fact that he can't retain the lines. He thinks he's not regarded highly enough to deserve a dresser. Salary, for another.

BERNIE: Why salary?

GEORGIE, *shrugging:* He's learned that Mabel Beck is earning more. In fairness to him, the figure is low for the part.

BERNIE, *archly:* The figure's fair. Not great, but fair.

GEORGIE: Granted, but not to him.

Bernie pauses; they both are beginning to tighten.

BERNIE: What was his last salary? And what year was it earned?

GEORGIE: If you thought enough of Frank to give him the part —and you did!—isn't that a very silly remark?

BERNIE, *coldly:* I happen to have other plans for Frank's financial participation in the show. If he works out—if the show runs—I make him a five per cent partner, as a gift.

GEORGIE, *hesitantly:* Would you give him that in writing?

BERNIE, *angrily jumping up:* No, I won't give you that in writing!

GEORGIE, *pallidly:* It would help him if you did. Tomorrow— this week, staring probable bad reviews in the face . . .

BERNIE, *eying her:* You're clever—don't overplay your hand. Let's face it. Frank may go anywhere from here, even to a wealthy movie career. Or he may go right back to the gutter, and you right with him!

GEORGIE: Do you think that was called for?

BERNIE: Just like you, I don't always say and do what's "called for."

GEORGIE, *puzzled, hurt, wary, trying to understand:* I don't mind you being angry if I know why—

BERNIE, *flaring:* I have no problems with Frank—don't you make them where they don't exist! *He swings away.* I could almost love a woman like you. My motto is "No pity!" too!

GEORGIE: I wonder if you'd be kind enough to give me the code. What're you talking about?

She has turned, careful and restricted. Invited, as it were, he comes down from the door and stands behind her, almost enjoying this moment.

BERNIE: Here's the code. I'm ambitious—I wanna get *my* picture on a green postage stamp, too. There's a difference between us, of course. Way up on the twenty-fourth floor is where I live. And sometimes, late at night, I look out way over the sleeping city and think how I'd like to change the history of the world. I know I won't—the idea is talented but phony. I admit I'm a gifted mountebank. What are you? Do you know? Do you admit it, even to yourself?

GEORGIE: What am I?

BERNIE: Lady, you ride that man like a broom! You're a bitch!

GEORGIE, *after a long moment:* You have a very lyric and lurid opinion of me.

BERNIE, *rapidly, dropping his voice:* Now, be careful, Mrs. E. It's a bitter mess for me if Frank fails. But I can hire other actors. I doubt if Frank can hire another director.

GEORGIE: I had no idea you were this tense tonight.

BERNIE: I'd tell you these same things any other night.

GEORGIE, *stronger:* Yes, you would. You have the bloody eye of a man who smokes too much. Tobacco's a drug—it warps your judgment. I'll have to remember that.

BERNIE, *sardonically:* I have to go stroke some more of my tender chicks.

Georgie stands there in proud, helpless silence, deeply hurt. Bernie walks to the door. Frank, in an exuberant mood, opens it and bumps into Bernie.

FRANK: Shut my mouth, the traffic's bad tonight! Well, that spot's all cleaned up! Bernie, that line mix up—it was the kid's fault all the time!

BERNIE: Be back in two minutes—have to give Mabel Beck some notes. By the way, Frank, does it bother you to have the understudy hanging around?

FRANK, *heartily:* Me? Why in hell would a Lucas bother an Elgin? Never even heard of the watch! Ha! Ha! Ha!

Bernie cocks a quick smart eye at Georgie, then goes. Frank ripples on like a happy river, washing and dressing quickly.

FRANK: Georgie, that line mix up—it was the kid's fault all the time! We'll get a load of fresh air in our lungs—I'll be dressed in a jiffy. How about a walk right across the Common?

Humming his happy snatch of tune, Frank does not see, as we do, that Georgie, who has moved to the trunk across the room, is trying to hold back tears. Frank dresses and chatters on happily.

FRANK: Guess what I'm in the mood for? One of those one dozen oyster stews, half and half—just what the doctor ordered! Oh, boy, what that'll do for my stomach! What did that Cook say after I left?

Unable to speak, Georgie merely shakes her head. Frank half turns.

FRANK: What? Huh?

GEORGIE: You're getting a dresser next week. *She restrains her tears.*

FRANK, *practically exultant:* Really? Georgie, you beat the band! Can't live without me! I'll betcha Bernie was on my side!

GEORGIE: Yes.

FRANK: Look at me, just look at me! I'm winging like a lark!

GEORGIE, *half turning:* Frank, I wonder if I shouldn't go back to New York soon. You're getting a dresser now, and I think I'll be in the way. They resent me here and—

FRANK: What are you talking about? Are you kidding? Who resents you?

He starts toward her; the lark is grounded now. Turned away, Georgie abruptly bursts into tears. Frank stops dead, baffled and frightened. Only slowly does he move toward her with the shuffling gait of guilt.

FRANK: Why, darling, what's the matter? What is it, dear? Come on now, tell Poppa. What is it? He has turned her and has her in his arms.*

GEORGIE: I really must . . . get these teeth fixed . . .

FRANK, *relieved, with fond and rough sympathy:* Honey, why don't you tell me when something's on your mind? We'll get you a good dentist in the morning. *He starts toward the make-up shelf.* Here, take some aspirin.

GEORGIE, *stopping him:* No, I took a few.

FRANK, *comes back again, all sympathy, about to kiss and embrace her:* Darling, don't you know this is gonna be a honeymoon, up here in Boston?

GEORGIE, *as she pulls away and sits, with a bite of bitterness:* Yes, we all love each other, don't we?

FRANK: Boy, I'll never understand your moods, and that's the truth! A man can't be right, can he? Two strikes against him before he opens his mouth!

Sullen and offended, he goes back to his dressing. She sits, stiff, cold, and wordless.

FRANK: Now my stomach's all in a whirl again. That's what you wanted, isn't it? *He sits at the make-up shelf; there is silence and distance between them.*

GEORGIE: One day soon . . . we'll see what I want . . .

Curtain

ACT TWO: *Scene 1*

>>>->>>->>>->>>->>>->>>->>>->>>->>>->>>->>>->>>->>>-<<<-<<<-<<<-<<<-<<<-<<<-<<<-<<<-<<<-<<<-<<<-<<<-<<<-<<<

Frank's dressing room several nights later. It is past one o'clock in the morning, a cold, depressing time. They are taking photographs of the production onstage. Georgie is sitting on a chair, knitting. Paul Unger, on the couch, is pecking away on a portable typewriter. Georgie, wearing a coat over her shoulders, is tired and depressed but is covering it with a certain brightness and an excess of interest in what actually does not interest her. The radio is playing softly. After a time Georgie, chewing gum, looks up from her knitting.

GEORGIE: I wish they'd get finished out there.

UNGER, *hiding a yawn:* I've seen them take all night to photograph a show.

GEORGIE: Uhh! I've dropped a stitch! *Carefully:* Stitch, stitch . . . Makes me think of Hood's poem "The Song of the Shirt."

UNGER: You're very well read. I've noticed that before.

GEORGIE, *smiling:* What else could I do? My father was always away on tour, my mother was off with gardening and hobbies. *She sighs.* I do wish they'd get finished out there.

UNGER: I've seen them take all night to photograph a show. Didn't I just say that? Groggy!

Unger usually talks with a certain wry drollery and exaggeration because he is shy. Now he suppresses a yawn. Georgie also suppresses a yawn as she looks at a watch.

73

GEORGIE: Well, it's twenty after one. *Musingly:* When you think about it—so many plays and books, so much reading in the stillness of the night—and for all of it, what?

Unger stops his typing and looks over at her quizzically.

UNGER: The moment I saw you, Mrs. Elgin—the day I met you—I was touched.

GEORGIE, *turning, with a moue:* Golly, you mean I'm touching?

UNGER: Tell me—why did Frank begin to drink?

GEORGIE: There's no one reason a man becomes a drinker. You should know that—you're a writer, Mr. Unger. Looking back, I'd say bad judgment started him off. He had some money once, but you don't know my Frank—he wanted to be his own producer—eighty thousand went in fifteen months, most of it on two bad shows. I didn't know a thing about it— he was afraid to tell me. A year later we lost our little girl. It was awesome how he went for the bottle. He just didn't stop after that. You know what the theater is—give a dog a bad name . . .

UNGER, *quickly, as she turns:* Excuse me, I didn't mean to yawn.

GEORGIE, *smiling:* Let's make a pact, Mr. Unger—let's both yawn right out loud. *Impatiently:* Bernardo wasn't back to-night, was he?

UNGER: You don't like Bernie, do you?

GEORGIE: What's wrong with him? His wife?

UNGER: Among other things. But don't let that bluster fool you—he's actually a very innocent kid.

GEORGIE, *scoffingly:* Oh, sure, of course, why not.

UNGER: No, I mean it. Despite the talent, he's a dumb inno-cent kid in more ways than one. He's in love with art, for instance, and would make it a felony that you are not. But, as I say, there's more than popcorn in that head. Does my typing bother you?

GEORGIE: No. Does the music?

Unger shakes his head, decides to pack his belongings and go. She meanwhile has restlessly crossed the room and is sipping coffee from a container.

GEORGIE: Frank should be in bed with his cold. What did *you* think of the opening last night? Were Frank's bad write-ups justified?

UNGER: Man is to man as the wolf—they were not!

GEORGIE, *hesitantly:* Would you tell that to Frank? Make him feel good—he's low tonight.

UNGER, *massaging a kink:* Sure I will.

GEORGIE, *looking out of the doorway:* Why do you work in a dressing room?

UNGER: Frank's anxious about the new scene. And hotel rooms are very lonely.

GEORGIE, *turning:* You're young to have found that out.

UNGER, *grinning:* As a friend, Mrs. Elgin, that's a conceit with you—to talk like a veteran of all the wars. Actually, you're a young, very attractive woman. As for me, I'll talk big. This is my third play. Loneliness is the badge of the writer's profes-sion. It's ruined more good writers than every other reason combined.

GEORGIE, *crossing back to the make-up shelf:* Am I as attrac-tive as your aunt?

UNGER: Sue? She's almost as old as Frank. Very decent. My uncle left her cash, much cash.

GEORGIE, *delicately:* You could do something else for Frank. Ask her to have him out to lunch—it's a depressing week for him.

UNGER: Can do.

Frank hurries in. He has a bad head cold and is hiding a gnawing, nervous anxiety with affability and bluffness.

FRANK: How's that new scene going, sonny boy?

UNGER: I'll write you out of the play if that's all the respect I get!

FRANK: Well, two more scenes to photograph and we can walk. *Moving around the room, he stops at the make-up shelf:* Where's that cough syrup?

GEORGIE: It would bite you if it had teeth.

The bottle is right under his hand, on the shelf. He takes a quick swig and looks around, as if bewildered.

FRANK: Lemme see—what in hell do I wear next?

GEORGIE: Just the smoking jacket. *She crosses and gets it for him.*

FRANK: Bernie hasn't been around yet? *To Unger:* How *about* the new scene?

UNGER: I won't get to bed till it's finished. Bernie wants to put it in tomorrow.

Dressing, Frank thinks about this. Then he bends and picks up a newspaper clipping with a snort and chuckle.

FRANK: Yum yum! Did you see this notice? He claims I should have stayed retired!

UNGER: Forget those notices, Frank—they don't mean a damn!

GEORGIE: Frank, don't smoke any more.

Frank drops a cigarette he was about to light.

UNGER: How's your cold?

FRANK, *grimacing:* Tutti-frutti! Are we losing you?

GEORGIE: I wish they'd get through out there.

UNGER: Intuition tells me to get back to the hotel—it's very close back here. *He hefts the typewriter case.* It is generally supposed that I own this machine, but *it* owns *me*, body and soul—a form of depravity! Good night. *He drifts out wearily, Georgie murmuring "Good night."*

FRANK: Good night, baby. I like that boy. Nice boy—not a speck of ego in him. I have to have a cigarette, Georgie. I'm nervous . . .

Georgie says nothing. Frank lights a cigarette and takes another gulp from the syrup bottle; his nerves and anxiety show through now.

GEORGIE, *quietly:* I don't like that cough mixture you bought yourself.

FRANK: Why? It's a buck a bottle.

GEORGIE: A "buck a bottle" is a jim-dandy slogan, but you can read labels as well as the next one. Twenty-two per cent alcohol.

FRANK: Just leave it to me, dear. You know Poppa—walks like a mountain goat—never slips.

GEORGIE: Let me straighten your tie, mountain goat. *He comes to her dutifully, holds up his chin.* You're naughty, Frank.

FRANK: You get some more sleeping pills?

GEORGIE: Yes. Don't twist.

FRANK: Red or yellow?

GEORGIE: Red, but all you get is one.

FRANK: How about the blue ones? I hear they *really* knock you down.

GEORGIE: Why don't we have a party some night? We'll start with the red ones in chicken broth. Then . . .

Laughing lightly, she steps back, the tie fixed. But he abruptly takes her arms with a frightening intensity.

FRANK: Come here, Georgie . . . You're tired, too. Poppa's little helper. Go back to the hotel—we might be here another hour.

GEORGIE: I've waited this long . . . *She watches him as he goes and looks at himself in the mirror.*

FRANK: Look at that glass, will ya? Anything fits me! *Then:* Cook didn't come back, did he?

GEORGIE: No. Frank . . . ? What's the matter?

FRANK, *flaring:* Why in hell didn't Bernie come back tonight?

GEORGIE, *minimizingly:* Does he have to run back after every show to hold your hand?

FRANK: This is only the second night, that's all! What're you saying "every show"!

She watches him carefully as he turns away.

FRANK, *slowly:* They wouldn't spend all that money taking photos, would they, if they were considering cast changes? *Defiantly:* But I'm glad I got that two weeks' clause. And that's the truth!

GEORGIE: The pluperfect truth?

FRANK, *bitterly:* The pluperfect truth! I'll hand in my notice! Why should I care—do they? Producer and director don't come back the second night of a show!

GEORGIE, *quietly:* God is just where He was before . . .

FRANK, *whirling around:* How do I know if I'm good? Can't you understand how I feel?

GEORGIE: Yes, I can. I think you're really agonized. But one thing is gospel, Frank: If you walk off *this* show, too, you'll never see me again.

FRANK: Yes, ma'am, take their part—never mind what I'm feeling—take their part!

GEORGIE, *with quiet incisiveness:* This year I'm taking my own part.

Her tone seems to frighten him, for he stops and goes to the mirror and daubs at his face with a puff. Finally he makes a morose attempt at humor.

FRANK: Why'd you ever marry me?

GEORGIE: That's easy: you always had a box of Chiclets in your pocket.

He snorts and picks up several letters.

FRANK, *reading one:* How do you like it? Fan mail—three of them—all jail bait. "Have always wanted to be in the theater. Am seventeen and think I have the talent." Jealous? *She smiles. He tears up the mail and throws it in the basket.* No, it wouldn't matter to you, would it, if I took out a gal?

She smiles inscrutably. She knows Frank wants to recoup position, that actually he is trying to taunt her into a response of jealousy, affection, and regard.

FRANK: Well, would it? Would you care if I didn't show up some night?

GEORGIE: I'm not exactly taking sealed bids, Frank.

Frank answers a knock at the door with "Yes?" Larry looks in.

LARRY: We're ready, Frank, whenever you are.

FRANK: I'll be right there, Larry.

Larry nods and goes. Frank, sheepish, doesn't quite know what to say to Georgie. He slips the bottle into his smoking jacket pocket.

FRANK: Wanna come out and watch them take a few of these archive specials?

GEORGIE: No, it's cold out there.

FRANK, *contritely, crossing to her:* Mad at Poppa? *She shakes her head.* Not even if we go back to the same life, same room . . . ?

GEORGIE: People don't go back to the same life, Frank. They go above it or below it, but they don't go back.

FRANK: But do I still have the country girl?

GEORGIE: Here I am.

FRANK: I appreciate you, dear. Don't wanna lose you. But I hope you know that if not for me, you'd still be on the vine, in Hartford. *He starts out.*

GEORGIE, *nodding, moves toward him:* A toadstool in the woods. Here, take these tissues—you'll need them.

They meet in the middle of the room, each holding on to an end of the tissues.

FRANK: Thanks.

GEORGIE: And, Frank, leave the bottle here.

FRANK: I need it, dear.

GEORGIE, *quietly:* Over thirty years of know-how? Leave the bottle here.

FRANK: Georgie, I need it. *Abruptly fierce but hushed:* I need it!

He jerks the tissues out of her hand and walks out. Alone, Georgie shows that she is tired; she stands shyly, inward for the moment, head turned to one side. There is something very sad and lonely about her. Backstage hubbub is heard outside the door. Nancy enters, dressed in a bouffant evening gown. Life is a long, delicious time to Nancy.

NANCY: Mrs. Elgin, may I use your pier glass a sec?

GEORGIE: Pier glass? Haven't heard that phrase since I was a girl.

Nancy postures at the glass. Georgie smiles.

NANCY: Don't all people call this a pier glass?

GEORGIE: Only old ladies like me. Why, I go so far back I call rhubarb a pie-plant.

NANCY: But you don't! I can't bear it!

GEORGIE: I do.

NANCY, *giggles as she examines her beautiful self:* It's a beautiful dress, isn't it? My mother'll have kittens when she sees how low it's cut. *Sighing but examining still:* Oh, Mrs. Elgin, do you think I'll ever grow up? *Really* grow up?

GEORGIE: I know someone who wishes she hadn't.

NANCY: But you have no idea of what it means to be called "sweet child" or "Nancykins" by everyone and his brother!

GEORGIE, *dryly:* Yes, that can hurt.

NANCY: May I be forward? How old are you?

GEORGIE, *smiling:* On the dim, mysterious other side of thirty.

NANCY: That's old, isn't it? But look at you—we could be sisters!

Nancy has taken Georgie by the hand; arms around each other's waists, they look in the mirror.

GEORGIE, *sadly:* Cherish your puppy fat, dear. It's a passport to the best of life.

LARRY'S VOICE: Nancy Stoddard!

NANCY, *calling:* Here!

LARRY, *looking in:* Hey, you're wanted onstage, Nancykins.

NANCY: See what I mean? I can't bear it! Now you see why I'm so introvert!

Despairing, she rushes off in a flurry. Georgie remains standing at the mirror; she takes off her glasses and looks at herself. Something poignant reaches out from image to reality. The radio has begun playing a waltz. Georgie begins to sway to its rhythm, and in another moment she is waltzing alone, almost as if it were possible to waltz herself back to a better time. What she is murmuring to herself we cannot hear. Then she stops abruptly. A sardonic Bernie stands in the doorway.

BERNIE: Excuse me, the both of you. *He steps into the room.*

GEORGIE, *crossing to the make-up shelf:* Some aspirin . . . a headache.

BERNIE, *extends an aspirin tin taken from his pocket:* It's the Age of Aspirin, they say.

She puts on her glasses, gets some water, and swallows. Finally she turns.

GEORGIE: A splitting headache . . . too much stuffy dressing room . . .

BERNIE: Where's Frank?

GEORGIE: Onstage. *As he starts out she stops him, now in control.* His cold is getting worse, Mr. Dodd. He shouldn't be kept up this late. It's more than flesh and blood can stand.

BERNIE: Them's melodramatic words. We need production pictures, don't we? How's his spirit?

GEORGIE: Low.

BERNIE: The show's in fair shape—why?

GEORGIE: Ask the Boston critics. Everyone doesn't have your confidence.

BERNIE, *promptly:* That's true.

GEORGIE: And while I'm on the subject, that confidence makes you push. That makes you a bit of a bully.

BERNIE, *even more promptly:* That's true, too.

GEORGIE: Don't minimize what I say by agreeing with me— it's *really* true.

Tired, he looks at her with the typical curl of a smile and sits, almost as if to bait her, a way of releasing his own tension.

BERNIE: What else is bothering friend Frank?

GEORGIE: You didn't come back after the show tonight. Neither did Mr. Cook.

BERNIE: This last month I've spent from ten to fifteen hours a day with Frank. Nothing ever bothers him except through your mouth. Why?

GEORGIE: We've been through all of that before . . . *She closes the door and stops the radio.* He thinks it's a crime to lack a sense of humor. He doesn't want to be disliked. He hides when he's nervous. Either he jigs and jabbers away, or he sits in silence and rots away inside. But either way, for your edification, he's headed for a bender!

BERNIE, *mockingly:* Women always think they understand their men, don't they?

GEORGIE, *deliberately dimming her electricity:* I won't fight with you, Mr. Dodd. He expected you backstage tonight. Your absense was a reprimand. If you care at all for his sense of security—

BERNIE: Follow your advice?

GEORGIE, *looks at him as one wrestler looks at another:* Do you know anything about drinkers?

BERNIE: Something.

GEORGIE: If you're not careful, you'll have him full of whisky before he goes to bed tonight. He's got a bad cold. That's a respectable surface reason for any drinker to jump down the well.

BERNIE: Why work so hard at this marriage? Why not take a rest? You wear your husband down! You make him tense, uneasy. You don't stop "handling" him. You try to "handle" me, too.

GEORGIE, *in a flash of temper:* And don't think I can't, after handling a cunning drunkard for ten years!

BERNIE, *quickly up on his feet:* Who the hell do you think you are? Secretary of State?

GEORGIE, *defiantly:* I'm a drunkard's wife.

BERNIE, *snorting:* Girlie, I have to give you credit, but—

GEORGIE, *quickly:* No compliments, Mr. Dodd!

BERNIE: But I'm going to fight you as hard as I can for this man!

GEORGIE, *smiling faintly:* Not too hard. I may let you have him.

BERNIE: No, you want him wholly dependent! Now let's not waste words. I—

GEORGIE: Oh, it's much too late for that.

BERNIE: I was married to one like you. Roughly half my weight—ninety-seven pounds. It took her two years—she sewed me up!

GEORGIE, *dryly:* Love is hell . . .

BERNIE: We'll leave it at that—joke ending. *He goes to the door and turns.* What a bitter pity you don't realize the size of your husband's talent!

GEORGIE: What have *you* given up for that talent?

BERNIE, *coming back:* Then why do you stay?

GEORGIE: Because he's helpless!

BERNIE: I'll help him!

GEORGIE: *You!* You wouldn't know where to begin. Life with him is three-quarters the avoidance of painful scenes. He's taught me to be a fish, to swim in any direction, including up, down, and sideways. Now, disregarding facts, you happen to think I wheedle his life away. You're very—

BERNIE, *unable to contain himself:* Look, look, look! Half the world's shamed by sentiment. Say "mother" or "babe," "sacrifice," and they drip like axle grease! But you have ruined this man—don't explain it away by sentiment!

GEORGIE, *incredulously:* How did I so overrate your intellect? You're a boy!

BERNIE: Man or boy, I'm putting on a show—it has to work! We can discuss universals some other day! To be frank, you are slightly grotesque to me, Mrs. Elgin!

GEORGIE, *bitterly:* And what about yourself? Look at you, fearful of failure, effective and hard-hitting—a machine, without manners or style—self-driven, curt, wary, and worried—pretending to a humanity you never practice!

BERNIE, *contemptuously:* You called your own husband a cunning drunkard?

GEORGIE, *flatly:* It is necessary for you to know it!

A pause. They are murdering each other with their eyes.

GEORGIE: This is getting stupid. Now tell me, in God's name, exactly what you want me to do for Frank. *She sits down at the make-up shelf.*

BERNIE, *pointing a finger at her:* That's fair! I'll believe everything you say. Prove it!

GEORGIE: How?

BERNIE: Get out of town! *He pauses.* I've just had a bad fight in the box office with Cook. He's got a first-class replacement for Frank and seventy thousand dollars to protect! Frank will improve every day—I think he will, Cook thinks he won't. Well, he won't, unless *you get out of town!*

Georgie thinks, stops, looks, and listens.

GEORGIE: Umm . . . I'll do it. I'll go back to New York. *She stops him from leaving.* But only on one condition: let *me* carefully tell Frank, in my own way, at my own time.

BERNIE: As long as you're on the train by tomorrow night, understand?

GEORGIE, *nodding:* Life is earnest, life is real, and so are investments—I understand. But you may be sorry.

BERNIE: You're as phony to me as an opera soprano!

Georgie abruptly slashes him across the face with her open hand.

GEORGIE, *fiercely:* Did I forget to tell you I'm proud? Someone has to stop you from calling me any name that pops into your little head!

BERNIE, *frigidly:* Maybe I deserved that. Maybe not. Time alone will tell.

GEORGIE: It brings all things, they say. *Holding back tears:* Thank God for *that* inevitability.

Frank opens the door before Bernie reaches it.

FRANK, *jovially:* Bernie, old boy, where you been all night? Every time I come in here—you and my wife—what gives?

BERNIE, *turning away:* How they doing out there?

FRANK, *chortling:* We're through! Georgie, we're through—called it a day! *To Bernie, cautiously:* But, baby, did you see the show tonight? *Bernie nods.* Well, give!

BERNIE: I'll tell you what a Harvard professor said—which is why I got back this late: "That man's extraordinary!"

Frank begins to change to street clothes. He puts the cough syrup on the shelf.

FRANK: Hear that, dear? We're in the colleges now!

BERNIE: What happened there in Act Two again?

FRANK: Bernie, it's that same damn thing, that same fast cue. Unger says it's all right to fix.

BERNIE: I don't see why not. *He makes a note.* I'd like to put the new scene in tomorrow. You tired?

FRANK, *scoffingly:* Who? Elgin, the actor who likes to be compared?

BERNIE: Your energy was low again tonight.

FRANK: Sure, it's this goddam cold.

Bernie begins to look searchingly at Frank. He is not stupid, and there may be a modicum of truth in what Georgie has said. She is on the other side of the room, bracing herself, ready to have the truth out at any cost.

BERNIE: Not nerves? *Warningly:* We're gonna begin bearing down now. How *is* the cold?

FRANK: Under control.

GEORGIE: Why don't you tell him what's bothering you?

FRANK, *rolling his eyes:* What's bothering me?

GEORGIE: Cook and the notices, for instance.

FRANK, *innocently, to Bernie:* I just wondered why he didn't come back, that's all. Is he mad? I mean, let's face it, they weren't exactly money notices.

Georgie is not to be shaken off this time, despite Frank's tacit warning that she keep quiet. She steps in. Bernie watches carefully.

GEORGIE: Frank, Mr. Dodd believes in you. I can't help you if you're worried—he can.

FRANK, *very firmly:* But I'm not worried. He's got his own headaches, dear.

BERNIE, *steps in, testing the situation:* Frank, you're a talent—I expect to pay for that. I don't expect you to be easy and convenient—I'm no fool. Now, does anything seriously bother you?

FRANK: Wouldn't I tell you if it did?

BERNIE: I think you would.

But Bernie still watches and probes. Georgie steps in sharply between the men.

GEORGIE: Did you or did you not tell me, ten minutes ago, right in this room, that you wanted to hand in your notice!

FRANK, *exploding:* Well, for crying out loud! If a man can't say anything in a gag! Have to watch my step—can't open my mouth no more!

He throws Bernie a long-suffering look. Stopped, Georgie purses her lips. Bernie deliberately throws another chemical into the brew.

BERNIE: Your wife says she's thinking of returning to New York.

GEORGIE: I told you nothing of the sort!

FRANK, *turns, alarmed and anxious, syrup bottle in one hand:*
What do you mean, New York?

GEORGIE, *deciding to take a new tack:* Yes . . . I might go back
to New York.

*Puzzled, worried, wary, and off balance, Frank is about to take
a swig of the syrup. Georgie lifts the bottle out of his hand
and bangs it down on the shelf behind her. Then she crosses
to her purse. Bernie starts to leave but turns abruptly and
picks up the bottle.*

BERNIE: What is this?

FRANK, *minimizingly:* Cough syrup. Pine, tar, cherries—a whole
bush in a bottle!

BERNIE: Do you know it's laced with twenty-two per cent alcohol?

FRANK: Alcohol? *Very surprised, pretending puzzlement, he
glances at the label. Glibly:* Yeah, there's alcohol in it, all
right. I asked Georgie to get me some stuff to loosen me up in
the chest, and this is what she brought me back.

BERNIE, *sternly but emotionalized:* What do you think you're
doing, Frank? My father was a drinker—he ended up under
subway wheels. I know what these little appetizers can do!

FRANK: Didn't even occur to me, Bernie. *Chidingly, to Georgie:*
Gee, dear, you wanna watch yourself on a thing like that.

*Bernie looks from Frank to Georgie. She is tired but un-
daunted.*

GEORGIE: Get dressed, Frank. I want to go home. I'll be waiting outside. *She walks out, taking her purse, closes the door.*

BERNIE: Frank, my problem is the show. She's jealous of the show and jealous of me. *He has taken the bottle and is pouring its contents down the sink.* This is how far she'd go—far enough to kick you off the wagon!

FRANK, *watches furtively and uneasily:* Bernie, I know she's high-strung and difficult, but I can't believe she'd—

BERNIE, *stops him by slamming the bottle into the metal waste basket; harshly:* I want her back in New York! We have hard work ahead! *He stops.* Frank, I wouldn't relish having to tell you . . . Go back to the hotel—get a good night's sleep. I want you fresh and clear—I'm putting the new scene in at one o'clock.

FRANK, *warily:* Yah . . .

Bernie opens the door and curtly calls, "Mrs. Elgin!" This makes Frank very uneasy. Georgie returns.

BERNIE, *tiredly:* Frank knows exactly how I feel. See you at one tomorrow, Frank.

FRANK: Good night.

Bernie goes, closing the door. Georgie is silent. Frank, full of childish guilt, doesn't know where to look. Georgie is tired, worn thin, doesn't need much to make her break through.

FRANK: Where's my cigarette? He can be very arrogant and insulting, can't he? *He waits.* Must be cold out.

GEORGIE: Clean up, Frank. I'm beat out and in no mood to socialize.

FRANK: He had no right to talk to you that way.

GEORGIE, *with some bitterness:* Did you tell him so?

FRANK: Georgie—he—I'm ashamed of myself . . . *He stands up, wiping his face quickly.* Give me two more minutes, dear.

She sits stiffly on the edge of a chair, not looking at him. He is working swiftly, changing his trousers. Slowly she looks up, turning her head this way and that.

GEORGIE: Frank . . .

He turns innocently; she is eying him cannily.

FRANK: Yes?

GEORGIE: Where's the other bottle?

FRANK: What bottle?

GEORGIE: I'm tired, Frank—don't play peek-a-boo. Do you have another bottle of that syrup?

FRANK: No, I don't.

GEORGIE, *standing:* Give it to me.

FRANK: But I didn't buy another bottle, dear.

A twisted, punished child, he stands there while her eyes roam from his face to the corners of the room. She crosses abruptly, pulling down a hatbox; finding nothing in the box, she goes through the pockets of a garment.

FRANK: Wish you'd take my word for something for a change.

She ignores his hushed protesting as she goes to the trunk and pulls out the top drawers in her search.

GEORGIE: What a night! What a night! And all the time there's been a clanging in my head. I don't know who's punishing who any more!

FRANK: I wish you'd take my word for a change . . .

GEORGIE, *abruptly:* Never mind! I give up—I'm not going to look! Where's my knitting?

She looks around, trying to locate both knitting and herself. When she finds the knitting bag under his clothes on the cot she brings it over to her purse on a chair. He is confused and humble, abject.

FRANK: Georgie, I wanna apologize, Georgie. He had no right to take that attitude.

GEORGIE: Didn't he? He has the right to take *any* attitude—in ten years he's the only friend you've had!

FRANK: Excepting you, dear! And that's what I want, dear, the chance to show you how much I love you!

She has difficulty putting on her coat—one sleeve is turned inside out, and this increases her frustration and anger.

GEORGIE: How much you *need* me, you mean!

Frank is now revealed in all his naked helplessness and agony.

FRANK: Please, Georgie, don't be mad at me. I know I'm no damn good, but I'm worried to death!

GEORGIE: Tell that to Bernardo!

FRANK: Think of what it means to me to walk out on that stage every night—the whole responsibility of the show is on my head!

GEORGIE: *Tell that to Bernardo!*

FRANK: Baby, I don't know where to hide—I'm ashamed! Don't know the old lines and tomorrow I get a big new scene! And now you say you're going back to New York—I can't do this if you don't help me! Did I ask them for this part? Didn't they come to me? Weren't you there when he came to me? They don't appreciate what I'm doing for them! They don't—

She cuts him off, changing his direction to one of heated indignation.

GEORGIE: Stop putting on a front!

FRANK: Who's putting on a front?

GEORGIE: *You're* putting on a front! And you lie, you lie!

FRANK, *flaring:* What can I do, whine and complain? You want me to make them hate me?

GEORGIE, *bitterly:* They'll adore you when you go off on a bender!

FRANK: Who says on a bender?

GEORGIE: Old waffle iron says! The mop behind the door . . . *She pauses, her eyes flooding despite herself.* This is how it ends, that *laughing dream*—you had a laughing dream, five weeks ago . . . *She takes a handkerchief from her purse and uses it on her nose.*

FRANK, *turns away, dressing and muttering to himself:* I don't know anybody up here in Boston . . . the whole company . . . none of them like me, not even Bernie. How do I know he's keeping me on? Did he act like a friend tonight? *He turns to her.* Are you going back to New York?

GEORGIE: I don't know why not.

FRANK: You wanna leave me, don't you?

GEORGIE: It's late, Frank—I have to wash some stockings—

FRANK, *stepping in:* Tell me! You do, don't you?

GEORGIE: I want to go to bed—I may have a happy dream!

FRANK: Who's in New York?

Georgie turns, looks questioningly at Frank.

FRANK, *harshly:* What pair of pants are you looking for?

GEORGIE, *outraged:* Frank, I warn you—I'll hit you with the first thing I pick up!

Face to face, they eye each other for a moment. Frank finally moves away to the clothes hooks but does not drop his voice.

FRANK: They all want me to fail! And you want me to fail, too! You don't love me!

GEORGIE, *wearily:* Come on, Frank.

FRANK: All I've got is two hands!

GEORGIE: Well, use them. It's two A.M.—you have a one o'clock call.

FRANK: If you're in such a big hurry, there's the door! I, as a matter of fact, may take myself a walk. Get myself a baked apple and some milk.

GEORGIE: Your cold is getting worse—

FRANK: Let *them* worry about it! And I told you what *you* can do!

GEORGIE, *everything hurting:* You want me to go? Is that what you want?

FRANK: If you're in such a hurry . . .

She looks at him and her face tightens; angrily she picks up her purse and knitting bag.

GEORGIE: Oh, the hell with it! Just the hell with it! I'm going back to the hotel—do what you want! Sometimes I think you're plain out of your head!

She exits without more ado, slamming the door hard. Frank whirls around; he glowers bitterly, snorting and mimicking her tone, walking in circles before he snatches his tie off a hook.

FRANK: Out of your mind! Do what you want . . . plain out of your mind! Your cold is getting worse! That's right—walk out on me! Typical! Typical! *He is down at the pier glass now, angrily snapping the tie into a knot, muttering to himself.* Forget I'm alive. Take their part and forget I'm alive! Helpmate, real helpmate . . .

He dribbles off, his attitude abruptly changing. He stops and then tiptoes to the closed door and listens. Then he goes to the trunk and from the bottom drawer brings out a full bottle of cough syrup. He uncaps it, takes a swig, and throws the cap away over one shoulder. The bottle plopped down on the chest in front of him, he continues with the tie and collar. His tone is less intense but as bitter.

FRANK: Helpmate! Sweetheart! Country girl!

Curtain

ACT TWO: *Scene 2*

》》-》》-》》-》》-》》-》》-》》-》》-》》-》》-》》-》X《-《《-《《-《《-《《-《《-《《-《《-《《-《《-《《-《

Frank's dressing room twelve hours later. It is early afternoon. The dressing room is dark. A sound of snoring is heard. There is a persistent knocking at the door now. Frank, who has been asleep, stirs on the couch. We are dimly aware that he is sitting up. The knocking persists, and a voice is heard.

VOICE: Is there anybody in there? Mr. Elgin?

The lights go on around the mirror. Frank has toddled over to the switch and stands there blinking. The knocking persists.

VOICE: Are you in there, Mr. Elgin? Frank?

The knocking stops and several voices are joined in conference outside the door. Frank realizes where he is and what is happening. He is fully clothed, including topcoat, and shows in everything the evidences of having been drunk. He mutters under his breath.

FRANK: Oh, my God . . . my God . . .

He does not know what to do first. He tries to brush his hair back with nervous hands; nothing will help him at this moment, particularly as he is being hunted and pushed by further knocking on the door.

VOICES, *including Larry, Cook, and Unger:* Is the key in there with you? Open up, Frank! Is the key in there with him?

FRANK, *looking around, realizes he is trapped, clears his throat:* Yes, yes . . . what is it?

VOICE: This is Larry, Mr. Elgin. May I come in?

FRANK: Yes, Larry, yes . . . just a moment, please . . . *Sotto voce:* Oh, my God . . .

He hangs up his coat; it slips to the floor. Shaking himself, dabbing pitifully at his face and hair, he finally opens the door. Larry and Cook are standing there, Unger behind them.

FRANK: What's wrong? What's wrong, boys?

They come in and look at him. Frank blusters, smiles crookedly.

FRANK: Well, where's the fire?

LARRY: It's past two o'clock, Mr. Elgin. Your door was locked and the key wasn't on the rack.

FRANK: I was napping in here. Tired.

He tries to light a cigarette, but his hands shake so that Larry quietly steps in and holds out a match for him.

COOK: There was a one o'clock call for the new scene!

FRANK: Ow-ow! Completely slipped my mind! Walked around. Got tired. Slept in here and just forgot—

COOK: You mean you "slept it off" in here! You're so loaded you can't stand straight right now!

LARRY, *restrainingly:* Mr. Cook . . .

Frank drops into a chair at the make-up shelf.

UNGER: What the dickens happened to you?

FRANK, *snarling:* Nothing happened to me! I have a cold! Had a couple of beers and some food— *He puts his head in his hands; the world is whirling for him.*

COOK } *together:* Look at him! Smells like the sovereign state of Kentucky in person!

UNGER } Where's Bernie?

LARRY: We've sent for him.

COOK, *fervidly:* Well, this does it! Thank my lucky stars this does it! That wife of yours can help you start packing!

Only Larry sees that Georgie has come in at the door. Head down, Frank does not see her.

LARRY: Mr. Cook, I can't let you talk to an actor that way.

COOK, *not believing his ears:* You can't what!

LARRY, *white-faced:* You're the boss, Mr. Cook, but you can't talk that way to an actor in any show I'm on. I won't permit it.

COOK: *You* won't permit it?

LARRY: There is a lady in the room, too. I'll have to ask you to keep quiet until Bernie gets here—

COOK, *grimly:* We'll see what he says when *he* gets here!

He walks out of the room. Unger follows him, after shaking his head dolefully at Georgie. Frank has not looked up. Larry approaches him in a kindly way.

LARRY: Can I get you some coffee, Frank?

Frank does not answer or lift his head.

GEORGIE: Don't get him coffee, Larry—it makes him sicker.

LARRY, *after a pause:* I'll get you a Bromo-Seltzer.

He looks at Georgie and leaves the room, closing the door. Georgie does not move.

GEORGIE: Where were you all night?

Frank stands and reels over to the couch. He falls to a sitting position there.

FRANK, *with averted eyes:* Get me some water. Let it run . . .

With a still face she crosses to the sink.

GEORGIE: It's not very cold . . . Watch that cigarette, Frank. You'll have us all on fire in a minute.

He drops the cigarette underfoot and grinds it dead.

FRANK, *bitterly:* I missed the reading and that's *all* I did miss! *She crosses and gives him the water.* Where's Bernie?

GEORGIE: I don't know.

She turns. Bernie has pushed the door open; he snaps on the room lights. Behind him are Cook and Unger. Frank drops his eyes, and his soul drops its head within. Bernie comes to the center of the room; he turns squarely, on a line with Georgie.

BERNIE, *in a low, tense voice:* When did you see your husband last, Mrs. Elgin?

GEORGIE, *eying him warily:* Past two this morning.

BERNIE: Where?

GEORGIE: In this room.

BERNIE: Did he go back to the hotel with you?

GEORGIE: No, he wanted to go for food. I was tired.

BERNIE: What did you tell me when I phoned you in your room today?

GEORGIE: You asked me where Frank was. I said I didn't know. You asked me if he'd had a good night's sleep. I hoped he had, I said.

BERNIE: Why did you lie?

This scene is so painful to Unger that he slips out.

GEORGIE: I am not aware, Mr. Dodd, that I lied!

BERNIE: You didn't think it was important to tell me that Frank hadn't been home all night?

GEORGIE: Suppose he'd been with another woman?

BERNIE: You're being deliberately evasive and childish!

A tap at the door, a voice saying, "It's Larry . . ." Bernie barks back without turning, "Wait outside!"

BERNIE: Where did you get him a bottle after midnight?

GEORGIE: Where did I—? *She is so astounded that she is unable to resist a strange, strained laugh.*

COOK: What the heck's so funny? I resent that!

BERNIE, *turning to him:* There's only one thing to do, Phil—

COOK: And, yes, sir, I'm going right out to the box office to do it! *He walks out quickly.*

BERNIE, *without looking at Georgie:* There is still one person too many in this room.

Georgie smiles faintly and walks out, closing the door.

BERNIE, *quietly:* What about this?

Head down, Frank does not answer. Bernie waits; and then we see that he is really very emotional about this incident, for now his voice vibrates.

BERNIE: I'm in a mood to cut my throat in public. God A'mighty, human beings are funny people . . . *He pauses, then abruptly harsh:* Sit up! Don't act as if I'm beating you up! Don't make me the victimizer! Sit up! *It seems for a moment that Bernie may hit Frank; instead he turns and walks away.*

FRANK: Don't bawl me out, Bernie. I'll stay till you get somebody else . . .

BERNIE: I'm tired right down to my bones . . . *Then, strongly, turning:* That wife of yours—she—!

FRANK: No, not my wife. Why kid around? It's all my fault—I'm no good.

This is said with such empty hopelessness that it activates Bernie once again.

BERNIE: You're guilty as hell! But I want you to do something for the kid—

FRANK: What kid?

BERNIE: *This* kid! Stop being naive: stop protecting her!

FRANK: Bernie, she's weak. She—

BERNIE: She's driven you to drink for ten years and you call her weak? You might be magnificent in this part, but it would have to start with her! She goes back to New York on the five-o-five!

FRANK, *weakly:* Bernie, kid, I can't leave her. Left her once—she cut her wrists. She'd cut her wrists again.

BERNIE, *angrily:* She goes back today!

FRANK, *in a nervous whisper:* Bernie, she's weak . . .

BERNIE: I'll talk to her. *If* we go on together, you move in with me for the duration!

FRANK: But Mr. Cook—he doesn't want me and—

BERNIE, *flashing:* I'm not so sure *I* want you!

FRANK, *fumblingly:* Bernie, you decide . . .

Bernie has gone to the door without even listening to Frank, who has not moved from his spot on the couch. Bernie crisply calls, "Mrs. Elgin!" When she enters she closes the door and goes directly to Frank with a fizzy drink.

GEORGIE: Take this . . . *He takes the glass but does not drink.*

Bernie begins talking from behind her. She turns to him, a wary hatred in her eyes.

BERNIE: Frank stays—you go! The management will take care of your expenses. Frank may follow you in a day or two— I'm not sure. Just now he's moving in with me.

GEORGIE: As crisp as lettuce, aren't you? You want me to go back, Frank? *Then, of his silence:* That means yes. I'll go and pack. *She crosses to go:* But I want to know one thing: why do you hold on to this sack of trouble?

BERNIE, *coldly:* I will answer that, for Frank's sake. I'm interested in theater, not show business. I could make a fortune in films, but that's show "biz" to me.

GEORGIE: What do you call this play, Literature?

BERNIE: That's true: it's show business, trying hard to be theater. And a man like Elgin, giving his best performance— he has the magic to transform a mere show to theater with a capital T!

GEORGIE, *quietly:* Let us hope . . .

With a sad smile she starts for the door, but Bernie steps up quickly, blocking her way.

BERNIE: One moment. Tell Frank he has nothing to worry about. *Georgie looks puzzled.* He thinks you may go drastic. It's happened before, I understand.

Frank turns, nervously murmuring, "Bernie . . ."

GEORGIE: What's happened before?

BERNIE: Phony suicide attempts.

FRANK, *nervously:* Bernie, she wants to help . . .

GEORGIE, *wearily, closing her eyes:* Mr. Dodd, we had a town idiot when I was a child. He kept insisting that elephants' tusks come from piano keys. You are very obtuse and willful, for a man who so relishes his own humanity.

BERNIE: What are you talking about?

FRANK, *weakly:* Bernie, she has to pack . . .

BERNIE: What are you trying to tell me, Mrs. Dodd?

GEORGIE: Don't call me Mrs. Dodd. Suicide attempts are Frank's department.

BERNIE, *walks back to the door, pauses, goes over to Frank:* Show me your wrists, Frank. *He waits.* Show me your wrists. *Louder:* I asked you to show me your wrists!

Agonized, Frank slowly raises his wrists. Bernie looks down for several intense seconds. The story is plain. Sickened, Bernie turns away, his face to the wall. Behind him Frank's head slips down into his hands; he sobs without control. Bernie slowly turns to look across at Georgie, who is on the other side of the room, face averted.

BERNIE: I must ask you several questions . . .

GEORGIE: Michael on angel wings couldn't talk to me with your face.

BERNIE: Frank may have to go back with you, unless you answer. He's been lying to me.

GEORGIE: He's incapable of the truth, as commonly understood.

BERNIE: You were "Miss America" in the late '30s?

GEORGIE: He told you that? *Then, turning, thinking:* Did I burn down a house in Great Neck? Or a hotel suite? Did I need a nurse to watch me while he was tending work?

BERNIE, *nodding:* Umm . . .

GEORGIE: You didn't recognize any of it, from the play you admired him in, *Werba's Millions?*

She slowly sits, the heart completely out of her. Frank has not lifted his face from his hands. Her eyes wet with tears, Georgie talks on, spent, scarcely knowing what she is saying.

GEORGIE: You don't know what it is . . . meet, marry, elope . . . nineteen, romantic, real cute, raised on too many books. Oh, my, I had such a naive belief in Frank's worldliness and competence. . . . Yes, I saw he drank. But that was only a pathetic hint of frailty in a wonderful, glowing man. It was touching and sweet—it made me love him more. He could reform— I'd do it for him. Well, finally, there wasn't much left to take over . . . *She pauses, turns.* Send him back to the hotel—he needs some rest.

Bernie hesitates before moving briskly to the door and calling for Larry, who immediately appears.

LARRY: Yes, Bernie?

BERNIE: Is Lucas out there? Is he "up" in Judge Murray's part?

LARRY: Yes, he is.

BERNIE: Could he go on tonight?

LARRY, *hesitantly*: Yes, I think he could.

Thinking to himself, Bernie murmurs, "Dunno what I'll do." Frank speaks, his eyes to the floor.

FRANK: I'll play if I get another chance . . .

BERNIE, *harshly, with a vicious jab of his thumb*: Take him back to the hotel! Dismiss the company—check with me around five!

LARRY: Yes, sir, Bernie.

Almost awed, Larry picks up Frank's coat. Frank stands slowly, looking at Georgie. She does not look at him.

GEORGIE, *quietly*: Go on, Frank. I won't leave without seeing you.

Frank takes his coat and leaves. Larry follows, closing the door. Silence. Bernie is tense and tender, smarting and apologetic. Georgie is abstracted and drained.

BERNIE, *finally*: May I smoke?

GEORGIE: May you smoke? What is that, homage to a lady? That will never make me forgive you, Mr. Dodd, for what you've said and done.

BERNIE, *pauses, not looking at her, not lighting the cigarette*: I'm very confused and troubled—what about Frank?

GEORGIE: Those lies are his big, respectable reason for having gone to pieces.

BERNIE: Why did he go to pieces?

GEORGIE: It needs an Einstein to tell you that.

BERNIE: I don't know where to begin apologizing, Mrs. Dodd.

GEORGIE: I'm a real lemon drop. You can begin by not calling me Mrs. Dodd. *Standing, she flicks him a look and begins buttoning her coat.*

BERNIE: Have you ever left him?

GEORGIE: Twice left, twice returned. He's a helpless child. *Wryly, lifting her purse:* Anyone taking a cab to New York?

BERNIE: But if he's as helpless as you say—

GEORGIE: He's not helpless now—he has you.

BERNIE, *earnestly, his voice quivering:* Listen, he has to be watched and handled. You can do that—no one else. I didn't know it before.

GEORGIE, *bitterly:* Then you've learned something—ripeness is all!

BERNIE: Listen, Georgie, if—

GEORGIE, *opening up:* I don't intend to stay! Even the cat's dragged me up and down the stairs in this theater!

BERNIE, *unhappily:* But the man needs you—he has to be watched!

GEORGIE, *turns from the door, and now he gets it:* You take on the job with waving banners and twelve hours later hand it back? YOU'RE TELLING ME! *She throws her purse on the couch and begins circling around him. Helpless, he makes an attempt here and there to stop her torrential anger.* Yes, he has to be watched—he has to be nursed, guarded, and coddled! But not by me, my very young friend!

BERNIE: Please—

GEORGIE: I'm going back to New York, to the fiesta of a quiet room. For the first time in twelve years I won't have to wonder where he is—he'll be in the strong, sober hands of Mr. Bernie Dodd!

BERNIE, *ineffectually:* Georgie, listen—

GEORGIE: Can you stand him up on his feet? Because that's where all my prayers have gone—to see that one holy hour when he can stand alone! *She avoids him as he tries to grab her.* And I might forgive even *you,* Mr. Dodd, if you can keep him up long enough for me to get out from under! All I want is my own name and a modest job to buy the sugar for my coffee!

BERNIE, *his temper slipping:* Wait—if you'll listen—!

GEORGIE, *evading him:* You can't believe that, can you, you goddam man! You can't believe a woman's crazy-out-of-her-mind to live alone! In one room! By herself!

Bernie is so aroused by her that he has grabbed her by one arm. She pulls away; he grabs with his other hand, whirls her around.

BERNIE: Dammit, listen to me! You're knocking all the apologies out of my head! *He has pulled her in close to him and is holding her by both arms.* Now, *listen,* Lady Brilliance: you have to stay—he doesn't play unless you stay! It's a time for promotion, not more execution! But I can't take the chance *if you don't stay!*

A quick tense moment follows. Georgie is frozen in his arms, her hands against his chest.

GEORGIE: Why are you holding me? *Pushing:* I said you are holding me!

Abruptly, not releasing her, he kisses her fully on the mouth. Then they both step apart and after a moment he walks to a chair and sits, turned from her.

GEORGIE, *thinly:* I . . . *She seems to come out of sleep.* What is that toughness of yours? A pose?

Bernie has not changed his position, except to put one hand over his eyes; it is some time before he can trust himself to speak.

GEORGIE: To be so mad at someone you didn't even know . . . ? No one has looked at me as a woman for years and years . . .

Bernie turns abruptly, facing her. She eyes his scowling face.

GEORGIE: You want to beat me up again, don't you?

BERNIE: No, I deserve anything you say—no excuses, no excuses . . . *His manner changes.* Now I need your answer. For Frank's sake, I want you to stay.

GEORGIE: Wanting, wanting, always wanting!

BERNIE, *humbly for him:* I'm asking . . .

A tap at the door, and Cook irritably bustles in.

COOK: Where are you, Bernie? I'm waiting. Ray Newton is on the phone—he's available. He can catch the sleeper and be here in the morning.

BERNIE: I'll be right there.

COOK: He's on the box-office phone.

BERNIE, *sharply:* I'll be right there.

Cook glowers quickly and goes. Bernie stands.

BERNIE: I have to go out now and battle him. He's armed with plenty of facts and weapons. Will you stay?

GEORGIE, *after a pause:* Yes.

He starts for the door, his face rigid. She stops him.

GEORGIE: You kissed me—don't let it give you any ideas, Mr. Dodd.

BERNIE, *quietly:* No, Mrs. Elgin.

He walks out, quietly closing the door. Georgie stands for a full moment, as if listening, an air of impenetrable unreality about her. Her hand slowly moves up to her face. Her fingers touch her lips.

Slow Curtain

ACT TWO: Scene 3

>>>->>>->>>->>>->>>->>>->>>->>>->>>->>>->>>->>>>->KK<-KK<-KK<-KK<-KK<-KK<-KK<-KK<-KK<-KK<-KK<-K

Frank's dressing room in a New York theater, five weeks later on opening night. A make-up shelf with a large mirror over it is at the left. A door opens directly onto the stage at the right. Georgie, as she is doing now, can stand in the doorway and listen to the play, which is in the second act. A stretch of dialogue can be heard from time to time; and later, when the curtain falls, the applause will be heard.

There is a hushed, tiptoe quality about everything. Ralph, Frank's dresser, enters, hangs a garment on the wall, and hands Georgie several telegrams.

RALPH: A few more telegrams.

GEORGIE: Thanks. How is it going on the other side of the stage?

RALPH: A big man, Mrs. Elgin, he's a big man—it's a positive honor to be working for him.

Georgie smiles. Ralph exits with a loaded powder puff. Georgie reaches for her glasses, leafs through the wires; one wire interests her and she doesn't see Bernie enter. When she turns she is startled to see him there. He is tense and nervous, all ears for the stage. He hangs his overcoat on a hook. He is in a strange and complex mood of cynicism and gloom, begrudging but not without hope, nervous and painful, with a quality of "riding" everyone and everything.

GEORGIE: Where've you been, Bernie, out front?

111

BERNIE: Out front. On an opening night, the world's most useless man.

GEORGIE: How is Frank?

BERNIE, *admitting nothing:* His first act wasn't bad. How's it been back here?

GEORGIE: Quiet. Mr. Cook came back but I wouldn't let him in.

Georgie puts a wire up on the mirror.

BERNIE: More telegrams?

GEORGIE: This one is from Mr. Unger's aunt.

Bernie strolls toward the make-up table. Georgie seems to evade him, going to the door and listening again. Bernie drops into the chair.

BERNIE: Why don't you go out front?

GEORGIE: On a New York opening night? Not me. I don't sit out there with all those nabobs and critics. I hear very well right from here.

BERNIE: That's the advantage of an onstage dressing room.

Larry appears in the doorway, a fierce workingman in shirt sleeves, minus his usual deference.

LARRY: Shh! Shh! Please! Quiet, dammit! Shh! *He goes without concession, closing the door.*

GEORGIE, *grimacing:* That's the *dis*advantage. *She crosses, worried.* Isn't Frank's performance pleasing you?

BERNIE, *annoyed:* He's erratic, in and out—the bursts aren't coming! We'll see . . .

GEORGIE: Don't let him see your long face when he comes off.

BERNIE, *with a mock bow:* State Department Sadie—I forgot.

GEORGIE: Depressed, aren't you?

BERNIE, *readily agreeing:* Depressed and mean. *He sighs and fiddles with a powder can.* Well, it's been a long nine weeks. A job is a home to a homeless man. Now the job is finished— where do I go from here? *He turns; wryly:* I'm told—it has been intimated to me—that you call me Bernardo the Great.

GEORGIE: Haven't you been a magician to Frank? To both of us, in fact?

Bernie gets up and crosses impatiently to get his coat.

BERNIE: He can thank *you* for anything that's happened.

GEORGIE, *sincerely:* No, he can thank *you*, Bernie.

BERNIE, *sourly:* Here we go, jockeying for position again. *He turns, abruptly tense.* Georgie, five weeks ago I kissed a woman, a married woman; and now I love a woman, a married woman, and don't know where to turn. *He takes her arms, his voice ardent but low.* Lady, lady, close to you this way . . .

GEORGIE, *gently:* Bernie . . .

BERNIE: Who knows what'll happen after tonight—rehearsals are over—I may never see you again!

GEORGIE: Bernie . . .

She holds him off, her hands to his chest. He desists, smiling wryly.

BERNIE: Okay. *Nervously he snaps his fingers.* I didn't say before, what this must mean to you. No matter what happens to this show tonight, he'll have offers galore. *He pauses.* Are you leaving him?

GEORGIE, *quietly:* Don't you think the subject can wait?

BERNIE, *flaring abruptly:* No, it happens to be on my mind!
You've been evading me for weeks!

GEORGIE: You're unregenerate, Bernie—you'll never change.
In a minute we'll be at each other's throats again.

*She has not spoken unkindly, but he is ready to push to a
fight, it would seem.*

BERNIE: I don't mind a fight about something real! You could
be a home for me—that's real!

*Abruptly he lapses gloomily into silence and sits on a stool.
Frank's voice is heard lifted in a scene.*

BERNIE: Excuse me for blowing my wig. I can't escape that
voice tonight—it follows me everywhere I go. *He smirks.*
Listen to him . . . he's ready to give that dark sterling silver
quality to the best available parts. He needs you, dear.

GEORGIE: You're Frank's friend—you're thinking of his future
—I like that. But what about mine?

BERNIE, *gloomily:* Right, right, only right. I can't tell you
what to do, can I? But how can a man be so disgruntled and
still live? *His face averted, he runs a nervous hand through his
hair.*

GEORGIE, *moves to him, sympathetically:* I hate to see you
this way, troubled, contrite—

BERNIE, *gets to his feet and moves away, harshly:* Lecture me
no lectures!

GEORGIE: Now, why don't you stop clenching your fists to
hide your tenderness and pity? *She smiles.* Put your eyes down
before they burn a hole in me.

BERNIE, *staring at her:* Are you leaving him?

GEORGIE: Don't be willful, dear. You see, you'll go on—

She stops, for Bernie has turned his head and is listening sharply to the stage play; then he bounds to the doorway, ears even bigger. Georgie joins him, not knowing what is wrong. They go out. The stage is empty for a minute. Offstage we hear running feet and excited whispers. Frank's voice has risen high, bellowing and angry. Bernie brings an excited, half-hysterical Nancy into the dressing room. The dresser appears in the doorway, waiting for orders.

BERNIE, *impatiently to Nancy:* Shh, quiet! What happened? Shh!

NANCY, *sobbing:* He began to hit me, Bernie, onstage. I can't bear it! I don't know what he's doing out there—he's even changed the lines!

BERNIE, *mordant and cutting:* Quiet, quiet, this is an opening night! *He turns; harshly:* Close the door, Ralph—get back to your job! *Ralph obeys.*

NANCY, *excitedly:* He's, he's—his eyes are red—he looks right at you and doesn't see you! He's—I began to cry—he took me and shook me like a doll!

BERNIE, *sharply:* Come on now, it didn't hurt that much! That's the scene!

NANCY: To shake me and slap me like that? And to change the lines? I didn't know what to answer him!

BERNIE: Don't raise your voice—the curtain is up.

Nancy sullenly rubs her smarting face. Georgie anxiously returns.

GEORGIE: Are you all right, dear?

NANCY: Yes, I'm all right, Mrs. Elgin, I'm all right . . .

BERNIE: Now stop sulking, Junior Miss—go up and change for your last act.

NANCY: Yes, I will, Bernie, I will. It was just such a shock, Mrs. Elgin.

GEORGIE: We understand, dear.

BERNIE: I hope that's the biggest shock you ever get. Go on, now.

Nancy goes to the door, wary of Bernie's mood.

BERNIE: Come here.

NANCY, *turning:* Me?

BERNIE: Come here . . .

Nancy slowly comes to him; unbending, Bernie kisses her unsmilingly. She is happy again.

BERNIE: Go up and change.

NANCY: Yes, I will, Bernie, yes . . . gee . . .

She goes. Scowling, Bernie goes to the door and looks out. Georgie follows him.

GEORGIE: It was spooky—he's wild out there—he almost knocked her down.

BERNIE, *impatiently:* I've been waiting *forty minutes* for that burst! If he can play scenes like that, let him do what he wants.

They stand at the door, listening. They can hear Frank.

BERNIE, *after a moment:* Here comes the curtain.

Out of sight the curtain comes down on the second act. The applause is strong. The sounds of swarming stagehands are heard. Bernie and Georgie step aside; Frank enters like a man in a perspiring trance, heavy and hoarse, keyed to the just completed scene.

FRANK: Close that window!

GEORGIE: There's no window in here.

Frank is breathing heavily, like a boxer between two late rounds. Bernie, waving Ralph away, closes the door.

FRANK: I'm dripping wet.

GEORGIE, *warily:* Get your clothes off.

Frank throws off her attentions with a lifted arm and, half sobbing, waves an embittered fist at the world.

FRANK: I couldn't hold myself back! Belted, belted! Did I hurt the kid? *He sees Bernie.* Bernie, I couldn't help it, Bernie! I started to go and I couldn't help it!

BERNIE: Sit down and take it easy.

GEORGIE: Sit down, Frank, sit down.

FRANK: I'm sorry, kid, forgive me—it just came out that way! That's what he should do there, the Judge—no one wants him, not even his grandchild! And suddenly I got the image— they're caging a lion—like you shove him in the face! Like they do in the circus, with chairs and brooms! And I couldn't hold it back . . .

BERNIE, *firmly:* I didn't want you to hold it back!

Exhausted, Frank sits down.

GEORGIE: Now get your jacket off.

Standing behind him, she peels off the dinner jacket and hangs it up. Intermission music starts. Frank takes off his collar and tie.

FRANK: This is limp. I'll need a fresh one . . . I hope I didn't hurt that kid.

BERNIE: Don't worry—she's fine.

FRANK, *sighing, relieved:* Well, nobody's sore at nobody then. Golly, I was wild out there for a minute. They made me sore out front, too—they're sitting on their hands.

BERNIE, *mordantly:* They may be very moved.

FRANK, *growling but pleased:* Don't kid the ugly man . . .

BERNIE, *soberly:* I'm not kidding—your performance can only be a big surprise.

FRANK: That's swell! I hope so! Say, did you see that hospital scene? She's good, that Mabel Beck! *He turns.* Here are some more wires. Someone must remember Poppa. Here's one from Sue Lewis: ". . . renewal of a great career. Am out front rooting. Much affection and regards . . ."

The wire seems to affect Frank in a strange way; he looks at Georgie furtively, something on his mind.

FRANK, *briskly:* Let's see, what am I wearing next?

GEORGIE: The smoking jacket, dear.

FRANK, *to Bernie:* Jo-jo, the dog-faced boy—I wish I had four hands. Well, as long as you excused me for going wild . . .

BERNIE, *starting for the door:* Keep going wild and I'll bless you in Macy's window. Here's Philip Cook, Esquire—he'll do *even more* than *I* will in Macy's window! Be back.

Bernie exits, leaving the newly arrived Cook in the room.

FRANK: How is it out front, Mr. Cook?

COOK: I only know what I read in the papers. How do you feel?

FRANK: Good, good—pluperfect good. *Seated, Frank is sipping milk at the make-up shelf.*

COOK: The reactions in the lobby are pretty good. You hungry?

FRANK: This? It's for my voice.

COOK, *uneasily:* Frank, a lot of things . . . are said in the heat and toil of the day. I hope you'll accept my apologies . . .

FRANK: Sure, we all know how those things can happen. *With a sudden thought, he turns.* Of course, you include my wife, too, in your apologies.

COOK, *quickly:* Of course, Mrs. Elgin, I include you, too—of course!

FRANK: Then start by taking your hat off—you're not at a smoker, Mr. Cook.

Cook is very thrown by this attitude. Georgie silently watches the scene.

FRANK: This is the first polite word you've had for either one of us. And I think I know why. You—

COOK: Frank, it's human—if we have to protect a show—naturally—

FRANK: You want me to sign a run-of-the-play contract before the morning papers are out, for half of what I'm worth.

COOK, *removing his hat:* I'm really very sorry, Frank, and you have to believe me on a thing like that. As to different contractual arrangements, it *was* on my mind. *He bows stiffly and slithers sideways out of the room.*

FRANK: I guess *that* put a pimple on his nose. *Suddenly alarmed:* I hope I didn't say too much . . .

GEORGIE, *laughing:* He thinks you're wonderful in the show, but he wouldn't have the grace to say so. Just you keep your self-respect, the way you have it out on that stage tonight. And remember, Frank, don't forget—it isn't necessary to be liked by every Tom, Dick, and Harry Truman, even if he's President!

She has brought his smoking jacket, and he stands and slips into it, humming his favorite little tune.

FRANK: You're a real scrapper—I've always admired your nerve.

GEORGIE: Still some shine on your face.

FRANK: I'll fix it. *Thoughtfully he goes to the mirror.* That was nice of Sue, that wire.

GEORGIE, *levelly:* Yes, it was . . . You're handsome tonight.

FRANK, *slowly, turning:* Am I? *Seriously:* Well, after tonight—catch this one and tuck it in your memory book—you'll never again have to ask why you married me.

GEORGIE, *quietly, as she puts a handkerchief in his pocket:* Won't I?

Bernie breaks into this serious moment. He taps on the door and enters. Frank turns for his collar.

BERNIE: Friend Mabel sends her love.

FRANK, *abruptly:* Don't wanna be a pest, kid, but can I show you something? No collar and tie—just a collar button.

BERNIE: You mean go on that way?

FRANK: Yes, that's the way they arrest him, without a collar—from collar button to collar button in thirty years! Get it?

BERNIE, *half smiling:* It's a real point—leave it in.

Ralph appears briefly in the doorway, saying, "They're ready, Mr. Elgin." Frank has gone back to the shelf and is fingering a telegram as he looks at himself in the mirror. Larry's call of "Places, places. Third Act, please. Places!" is heard outside. Then he is in the doorway.

LARRY: You ready, Frank?

FRANK: Yes, thanks, kid, all ready.

BERNIE, *grabbing Larry by the arm as he is about to go:* Larry, don't take the curtain up till they're all seated—the front rows in particular.

LARRY, *grinning:* If the front rows had the balcony's manners —what a world this could be! *He goes; his third act cry is heard as a distant echo for quite some time.*

FRANK, *turning, hesitantly nervous:* Georgie . . . I can be wrong most of the time . . . but any ideas you have, if you want to leave me—don't. *Bernie is about to leave, but Frank stops him by crossing over.* I'm deliberately talking in front of a third person. Maybe I should do it more often—sometimes it's a big relief to fall on your face in public. *To Georgie:* Am I wrong, Georgie? Aren't you setting up Sue Lewis to put in your place? Don't leave me, darling. Give me a chance. I love you . . .

Georgie pauses for her answer; one of her hands creeps up to the lapel of Frank's coat.

GEORGIE: Frank, I certainly didn't want to bring up any of this tonight. But you did—so let's have the whole truth. I married you for happiness, Frank. And, if necessary, I'll leave you for the same reason. Right now I don't know where I stand.

FRANK, *humbly:* You don't . . . ?

GEORGIE, *drops her hand and steps back a little, carefully picking her way:* No. Because neither of us has really changed. And yet I'm sure that both our lives are at some sort of turning point. There's some real new element of hope here—I don't know what. But I'm uncertain . . . and you, Frank, have to be strong enough to bear that uncertainty.

FRANK, *hushed:* I think I know what you mean.

Larry looks in just long enough to say, "We're waiting, Frank."

FRANK, *nervously:* They're waiting, dear. I—I don't know how to say this, but no matter what happens, you have saved me, Georgie—you and Bernie. *He kisses her, then pulls himself together.* I think I have a chance.

He turns and exits firmly. After a moment Bernie seems about to say something to Georgie, but she is moved and withdrawn.

BERNIE, *as he slips out, muttering:* I'd better show my face on stage a moment—rah-rah stuff.

Unger, wearing a dinner jacket, enters, almost brushing Bernie.

UNGER, *jubilantly:* Frank is magnificent! He's really showing me what my play is all about!

GEORGIE, *smiling:* He's onstage—they're going up.

UNGER: You don't look like a veteran of all the wars tonight! You must be damn proud! I know my aunt is—we're sitting together. She's showing all the proprietary interest of a mother hen.

GEORGIE, *quietly:* Give your aunt my regards.

UNGER: I will.

He goes over to her, wanting to kiss her or touch her hands. She attempts the same, but it is clumsy and fizzles out. He goes. Georgie slowly walks to the door; she is thoughtful and inward as she looks out. Bernie returns, his spirits slightly lifted. The intermission music dies away. Larry's cautioning voice is heard: "Quiet backstage, please, we're going up . . . quiet, please . . ."

BERNIE: Everything shipshape . . .

GEORGIE: It was sweet of you to send him all those wires.

BERNIE, *impassively:* Who told you?

GEORGIE: Guessed. How many did you send?

BERNIE: Nine or ten. And you?

GEORGIE: Four or five.

BERNIE: There she goes!

The curtain goes up. Georgie and Bernie are looking out. A strained pause is followed by a rumble of applause.

BERNIE, *mordantly:* Applauding a third act entrance—surprise follows surprise. Well, this is the act where he wraps up the show and walks off with the town. *He goes to get his topcoat from the hook.*

GEORGIE, *leaning against the doorjamb, to herself:* He's handsome tonight . . .

BERNIE, *turning to her:* I'll go out front and watch. Good night, Georgie.

GEORGIE, *crossing to the make-up shelf:* He'll come off dripping again . . .

Humming Frank's snatch of tune, she is picking up some tissues and a towel; when she turns, Bernie has moved in closer to her, almost forcibly making her aware of his presence.

BERNIE: Good night, Georgie.

They are face to face.

GEORGIE, *gently:* Good night, Bernardo.

BERNIE, *wryly:* I don't know . . . maybe a magician *does* live in this frail, foolish body, but he certainly can't work wonders for himself! You'll never leave him . . . *He has been fishing in a pocket; now he jerks his hand out, almost angrily it would seem.* I keep running out of cigarettes!

GEORGIE: You smoke too much.

BERNIE, *mockingly:* You are impertinent, Madame! *Longingly:* And steadfast. And loyal . . . reliable. I like that in a woman!

GEORGIE, *her hand on his arm:* Wrestle, Bernie. You may win a blessing. But stay unregenerate. Life knocks the sauciness out of us soon enough.

Lonely, arch, and rueful, he looks at her a moment before stepping in and kissing her lightly on the lips. Then he turns, throws his folded coat over one shoulder, and slowly leaves the room.

For a moment she wears a sad and yearning look; finally a towel in her hand calls her back to reality. She crosses and takes Frank's robe off the wall and starts for the door. Meanwhile Frank's stage voice is heard, playing a quiet but powerful scene. A thought makes Georgie stop. She goes back to the dressing shelf, takes down Sue's telegram, considers it quickly, comes to a decision, crumples it into a ball and throws it into the trash basket. Then, head up, she slowly walks out of the room with Frank's robe across one arm.

Slow Curtain

THE FIRST PERFORMANCE

LYCEUM THEATRE,
NEW YORK CITY
OPENING—FRIDAY EVENING, NOVEMBER 10, 1950

Dwight Deere Wiman
presents
The Strasberg and Odets Production

PAUL KELLY   UTA HAGEN

in

THE COUNTRY GIRL

A New Play by
Clifford Odets
with
Steven Hill

Staged by Mr. Odets

Settings and Lighting by Boris Aronson

Costumes by Anna Hill Johnstone

CAST
(In order of speaking)

BERNIE DODD .... Steven Hill
LARRY .... Peter Kass
PHIL COOK .... Louis Veda Quince
PAUL UNGER .... Joseph Sullivan
NANCY STODDARD .... Phyllis Love
FRANK ELGIN .... Paul Kelly
GEORGIE ELGIN .... Uta Hagen
RALPH .... Tony Albert